Public Economics and Finance

Edited by Bernur Açıkgöz

Published in London, United Kingdom

IntechOpen

Supporting open minds since 2005

Public Economics and Finance
http://dx.doi.org/10.5772/intechopen.77359
Edited by Bernur Açıkgöz

Contributors
Pina Puntillo, Guy Yakana Yombi, Mounton Chouaïbou, Yakana Agoume Lucie, Elif Ayşe İpek Şahin, Esra Dündar Aravacık, Sibel Aybarç

First published in London, United Kingdom, 2019 by IntechOpen
IntechOpen is the global imprint of INTECHOPEN LIMITED, registered in England and Wales, registration number: 11086078, The Shard, 25th floor, 32 London Bridge Street
London, SE19SG - United Kingdom
Printed in Croatia

British Library Cataloguing-in-Publication Data
A catalogue record for this book is available from the British Library

Additional hard and PDF copies can be obtained from orders@intechopen.com

Public Economics and Finance
Edited by Bernur Açıkgöz
p. cm.
Print ISBN 978-1-78984-794-9
Online ISBN 978-1-78984-795-6
eBook (PDF) ISBN 978-1-83962-428-5

For EU product safety concerns:
IN TECH d.o.o., Prolaz Marije Krucifikse Kozulić 3, 51000 Rijeka, Croatia, info@intechopen.com or visit our website at intechopen.com.

Meet the editor

Professor Dr. Bernur Açıkgöz was born in 1979 in Ankara. After attending Ankara Finance School, she continued her undergraduate studies at Dokuz Eylül University, Department of Finance. She received her master's degree in Financial Law from Dokuz Eylül University. In 2006, she was awarded her PhD degree from Dokuz Eylul University Department of Public Finance. Her PhD thesis covered the topics of poverty and development. Professor Dr. Bernur Açıkgöz has books, articles and papers on foreign direct investments, economic growth, panel econometrics, experimental economics and game theory. She is currently the head of the Public Finance Department at Izmir Katip Çelebi University. In addition, Açıkgöz teaches at the Department of International Trade and Finance at Izmir University of Economics.

Contents

Preface

In recent decades, the role of governments across the world has dramatically changed. Developments and changes in the social sphere have led to changes in social needs. Accordingly, problems and solutions are also changing. The Industrial Revolution that took place in the eighteenth century had an important effect not only in the economic field but also on social structure. Because of these effects, the perception of social problems has changed and the social expectations from the states have increased.

Government administrations from ancient times to the present day have needed continuous financing and have provided this funding from various sources. The process of social development required public borrowing for different purposes ranging from creating a consumer society to selling the surplus of developed countries to post-war human relations and from the financing of developing countries to the payment of debt. In the modern state perspective, the needs still constantly increase and therefore the state has to spend more to meet these needs.

In this study, the process of change and transformation on welfare states and social policies on a global scale is examined conceptually and historically. The study aims to contribute to the literature by including past and present findings as well as assumptions about the future. This study, which also focuses on the political, economic and social impacts and current reflections of borrowing in the context of public debt theory, emphasizes the transformation in the external debt structure in the globalization process. In another aspect of public economics and finance, this study also evaluates the contributions of new budgetary approaches classified as: (1) environment-friendly budgetary approach, (2) citizen-centered budgetary approach, (3) citizen's budget approach, (4) participatory budget approach, and (5) gender-responsive budgeting approach.

Bernur Açıkgöz
Izmir Katip Celebi University,
Department of Economics,
Turkey

Section 1

Public Economics and Finance

Chapter 1

Social Policy and the Welfare State

Esra Dundar Aravacik

Abstract

The developments and changes in the social life have led to change in the social needs. Therefore, problems and their solutions also change. The industrial revolution which realized in the eighteenth century had some important impacts not only on the economic life but also on social structure. It was aimed to solve social problems and ensure prosperity through social policies, which is a multidisciplinary field, and consequently, the concept of welfare state emerged. The states, which had liberal concerns and traditional protection functions and reached a powerful position with their internationalist approaches, underwent a transformation period because of the economic and social developments which took place in the last quarter of the twentieth century. It has been subject of criticism that states increased the social expenses to satisfy the social needs and therefore caused an economic crisis in this period when the effects of globalization were discussed. In this study, the change and transformation process in the welfare states and their social policies at the global scale will be handled conceptually and from the historical development perspective. Making determinations about the past and present, as well as having assumptions for future, this study aims to contribute to literature.

Keywords: social policy, welfare state, globalization, welfare, social welfare

1. Introduction

Social policy is an inclusive disciplinary, which means to provide solutions to address needs of social life. Social problems change based on economic and environmental factors. These changes also differ based on social structure and state policies.

The historical background of social policies is in parallel with important events in the human history. An important cornerstone in the world history, industrial revolution, is an economic revolution on one side, but it increased the social problems on the other side. From industrial perspective, societies can be regarded as preindustrial society, industrial society, and postindustrial society. It is also possible to say that social policies that provided solutions to social problems also changed based on the conditions of the period.

It is seen that traditional methods were used to satisfy social needs, and the groups in need of protection were tried to be protected through social aid and services in the preindustrial period.

The period which began with the industrial revolution caused varied social problems as from the second half of eighteenth century. Seeking solutions to address the poverty and social imbalance, which were caused by the industrialization, social policy tried to make balance between economy and social policies. The migrations to industrialized regions with the impact of industrialization caused new professions, negative life and work conditions, and poverty. In the face of this change in the demographic structure, states adopted the liberal economic understanding as a solution. Free market economy that emerged as a result of concerns that state interventions would damage economic and social balances helped a part of society to have welfare but caused workers who constituted the majority of society to impoverish. Liberal economy understanding's failure to ensure social welfare resulted in criticisms and the rise of neoliberal approaches.

The fact that liberal state understanding's limited approach caused negative results on social policies led adopting a more interventionist and regulating state model. Because social expectations that the state should meet social needs increased, the state got a new character to solve social problems. Affected by the wars which broke out in the first half of twentieth century and 1929 economic crisis, the concept of state changed in favor of social policies. With Keynesian economic approach, it paved the way for more inclusive interventions and adopted "welfare state" approach. However, also affected by globalization, the interventionist approach of welfare state to ensure economic and social welfare failed to ensure economic growth, and the position of state was discussed again.

In this new period, where the increase of social expenditures and taxes was perceived as a threat, it was suggested that the social responsibilities of the state should be reduced. The crises beginning in 1970s and the problems which increased with the effect of globalization led to a transformation in the welfare state. The crisis of welfare state and the constantly increasing discussion about the role of state to determine social policies caused states to plunge into new quests.

Although the quests for the welfare state of Golden Age were different, it is possible to say that the basic attitudes were neoliberal attitudes like increasing the effectiveness of local administrations, leaving ensuring welfare ton on profit organizations, and leaving social services to private sector. Therefore, the Welfare State mode that emerged with industrial revolution was restructured with the "Information Age" and globalization which emerged in the last quarter of twentieth century. In this period, social policies are determined by civil society, international, and supranational organizations instead of traditional means, and social policy understanding turns into new forms.

In spite of all criticisms, welfare state still regulates and implements social policies today. Exposed to some transformations and to some extent replaced by neoliberal policies as a result of changes caused by the globalization and information age, the welfare state is predicted to continue its existence in new forms and remains as an important power to regulate social policies in future.

In this study which has been made under the light of this information and predictions, first of all, the conceptual foundations, targets, and means of social policy will be explained with the factors which paved the way for its emergence in the historical process. After that, the concept of welfare state and the effects and events, which paved the way for its emergence, will be handled in the historical process. Welfare state crisis and globalization will be explained under different headings and determinations, and predictions will be made about today and future, discussing their impact on the social policy.

2. The subject of social policy

Social policy is referred to as "social policy" in Continental Europe, but it is referred to as "social welfare policy" in the North American literature. Some authors argue that these two concepts have the same meaning but some others argue that social policy is a frame concept which encompasses various policies, including social welfare policy [1].

Differences regarding the definition of social policy also arise from periodic conditions. To Wagner, social policy means the measurements taken by state to protect workers, while to Kessler, it means the movements and struggles of social class and state's attitude against this struggle. To Lauber, social policy is a set of measurements taken at national level in order to change and regulate the financial and cultural life conditions in a definite period of time. Albrech defines social policy as all measures and institutions that are taken to protect the part of society which is in need of economic protection and to ensure social security and peace [2]. Marshall defines social policy as a set of policies developed by state to ensure welfare in order that it obtains service and income. Hagenbuch asserts that social policy is an effort to make sure that individuals have minimum standards and opportunities.

In narrow sense, social policy is an attitude to address the disputes, imbalances, and conflict of interests between employers and employees and to ensure harmony between classes in capitalist systems [3–5]. In narrow sense, the aim of social policies is to find solutions for the problems emerging in industrials societies. From this perspective, it serves ensuring the social justice for ending the social inequalities that have been caused by the industrial revolution in social policy. In narrow sense, it represents the policies for making a balance between labor and capital because it encompasses only problems of worker and labor classes [6]. These policies also include the provision of social justice.

In narrow sense, political policy approaches the working life as the basic element that can explain the society. In this context, it also deals with issues such as wages, working conditions, trade unionism, and collective bargaining [7].

In a broad sense, the concept of social policy means comprehensive practices which address not only the problems and needs of working class but also those of the other segments of society [8]. With a definition from this perspective, it is possible to say social policy discipline addresses the problems of urbanization, environment, health, and education and those of all segments of society such as workers, the disabled, the elders, children, and immigrants. In a board sense, social policy emerged together with the concept of welfare state after World War II. Therefore, social policy includes health services, social security, city, environment, and struggling against unemployment and poverty that affect social welfare. In a broad sense, the final target of all these practices is to ensure social peace, social justice, and equality between different groups [9].

Social policy is determined on the basis of redistribution. The regulatory and distributive view of policies serves to ensure that everyone living in society has social freedoms and equal opportunities [10]. Ensuring the welfare of each individual is the main objective of the state and other organizations that are social policy practitioners.

The members of society have such needs as education, social security, health services, and housing. Social policy aims to ensure the welfare of individuals through legislative regulations. Because social policy is affected by social developments, it changes based on the needs of individuals. State makes new regulations based on needs. It is possible to make separate regulations for those who are in need of protection from social policy perspective for children and youth, for the disabled, for families with low income, and for the elders.

The factors which affect and determine social policy are not only the needs of society and individuals but also are ideological movements, crime rates, unemployment, media, politics, industrial groups, and violence, such economic factors as debit and recession and the nature of welfare state (social democratic, liberal, etc.) [11].

Social policy can be defined as an area consisting of decisions taken with the participation of many individuals and parties, which is put in force after the state determines its basis [12]. There is a mutual interaction between social policy and economic policies [3]. Thus, the development of a country is not possible only through economic growth but also by achieving a fair and balanced growth to solve social problems. From this perspective, the problems in economy and those in social policy need to be handled together.

2.1 Principles and concepts of social policy

To achieve its goals, social policy needs to have some principles regarding the policies it will determine.

The social policy, which is put in force by the state and other institutions, affects the welfare of society directly. A state's regulations regarding welfare need to be determined by analyzing its social policies. The subjects and basic principles related with social policies are social needs and social problems, equal rights and social justice, efficiency, equity and choice, altruism, reciprocity and obligation, and division, difference, and exclusion [13].

Welfare state should provide some rights to the people. These are elaborated below.

- **Equality:** Achieving equality underlies social policies. Resources need to be distributed fairly in order to achieve equality. Equality has different types: equal outcome, equal opportunity, or equal treatment.

- **Equal opportunity:** It means that equal groups should be treated equally. Equal opportunity needs to be given to people regardless of their sex or group. Moreover, all people must have the same opportunities in educational system or in the labor market.

- **Need:** Basic needs are food, caring, and housing. Needs are not limited, and it is not certain which needs should be covered by states.

- **Freedom and rights:** There are different types of rights. Civil rights mean the absence of arbitrary arrest and detention but having freedom to discuss any opinion. Social rights mean social welfare and social security, right to education. Political rights include voting and joining political parties and freedom to explain opinion in a democratic way.

All of these rights are provided by welfare state. The individuals who live in society are bound to state through the bond of citizenship. He/she has the right to request the state to which he/she is a citizen to make policies which pave the way to provide him/her the rights he/she has. From this perspective, the citizenship concept plays an important role in determining the state's obligations and rights of individuals as a part of social policies.

The main goal of social policies is to ensure that everyone in society lives in harmony, afar from conflicts. Thus, the target is to ensure social justice, social development, social balance, social integration, and social peace [7].

- Thanks to **social justice**, everyone in society will have equal rights in the face of equal risks. In this way, the inequalities and differences caused by the economic chances are eliminated. All the policies that ensure that everyone has fair opportunities with regard to income, taxes, wages, education, and social security contribute to the development of social justice.

- Ensuring the **social balance** is possible if everyone in society lives in harmony and balance. Therefore, social differences need to be reduced. Especially the differences and inequalities, with regard to opportunities, of the individuals living in different regions cause this balance and harmony to deteriorate. It is one of the main objectives of social policy practitioners to eliminate the differences regarding the development level and to ensure that everyone benefits from the same social services.

- **Social peace** is ensured through policies aimed at eliminating the factors that lead to the deterioration of the balance within the social structure. Especially in the capitalist system, the social differences created by the free market can hinder solidarity throughout the society. For the creation of a society dominated by harmony and reconciliation, policies should be implemented in order to eliminate the negative effects on the psychology of society.

- **Social integration** refers to the minimization of political and economic factors that negatively affect unity and solidarity in society. Education, culture, and moral values are issues that affect social resolution in this sense.

- Achieving the goal of **social democracy,** it is possible to protect the fundamental rights and freedoms of individuals in democratic order with the legal order in the framework of democratic freedoms. The goal of democracy must be achieved in order to protect the individuals' rights to work and participate.

2.2 History of social policy

The social policy, which is considered to have emerged as a result of the economic and social developments in the nineteenth century, started to become meaningful with the industrial revolution. As a result of the change in economic relations with the industrial revolution, social changes became inevitable. With the industrial revolution, increased production gave rise to the need for more labor. The dominance of capital owners on the labor market increased even further through the liberalization of trade.

In a period when the liberal market economy approach (Laissez-faire) was adopted, the dominant opinion was that government interventions would negatively affect the free market [14]. The belief that a market created without intervention would enrich the people, on the one hand, ensured the enrichment of the owners of capital and, on the other hand, caused the labor sector to become poor. The poverty faced by children and women hurts humanitarian feelings [15]. Increasing poverty during this period when no intervention was made to workers' wages and working conditions caused the social problems to increase and thus the rapid development of social policies.

As a result of liberal approach in the economy, two opposing sections have emerged in society: the bourgeois class who are the capital owners and working class who are the labor holders. The reduced of wages, poor working conditions, and long working hours have led to social problems in the labor class and to class conflicts. In the nineteenth century, social policies were applied to solve the social problems created by the liberal economy understanding of the state. Providing social peace and justice through the intervention of the state in the working life, working relations, and wages is inevitable.

With the social reform movements that began in England and Canada between 1880 and 1920, social policies turned into a descriptive approach from the prohibitive approach [1]. In this approach, the state was criticized that its role in the work life was limited and rigid, and it was suggested that the state should regulate social conditions in order to eliminate the negativities in the work life. In this period, there was an opinion that the role of the state in social policies should increase, in the capitalist developed countries, such as France, Germany, and the USA.

Consequently, the emergence of social policy in the modern sense is attributed to social conditions created by French Revolution in intellectual-political sphere and those created by industrial revolution in the social and economic spheres [16].

After World War II, liberal economic approaches in developed countries were abandoned, and Keynesian policy approach was adopted with the belief that the state should intervene in social policies. Another important factor in the adoption of this approach is the 1929 economic crisis and its negative consequences. After the industrial revolution, the scope of social policies expanded, and not only the problems of labor sector but also those of the whole society were addressed. All of the issues such as health services, elderly and child care, struggle against unemployment and poverty, participation of women in working life, protection of the environment, and gender discrimination became issues for which the state struggled under social policy.

3. Toward welfare state

The concept of welfare state emerged in 1930s and 1940s. Unlike the concept of state which was adopted during World War II and which aimed for providing sufficient money to cover the need of army in far, welfare state aims at providing social policy, health services and thus providing social needs [17].

Welfare state concept gains different aspects in different countries according to their cultural, social, political, and economic legacies and historical developments. Welfare state aims at providing welfare of the individual citizens. According to the demands of labor market and civil society, welfare state intervenes in the economy.

Although there are many definitions about the welfare state, Asa Brigg defines it as follows: "It is a kind of state in which consciously organized public power is used to reduce the role of market forces." It is accepted within the scope of the role of the welfare state to provide a minimum income guarantee to individuals and families, to facilitate the prevention of certain social risks, and to offer good living conditions to individuals in society through social welfare [18].

Another definition of the welfare state is that "it is a contemporary state understanding that undertakes the duty to ensure a fair income distribution, protect the groups and classes in need of protection, direct the social security practices and employment policies, practice the politicize to meet the basic requirements of society such as education, health, and housing and takes measures for regulating the working life, thanks to the tax and wage policies it follows" [19].

3.1 History of welfare state

The difficulties were faced with regard to making definition of the welfare state and justifying its historical development. As mentioned above, each and every state has a different national social security system, a different social structure, and thus, different needs. Moreover, welfare state determines the policies that are required by the economic, social, and cultural conditions and put in force the legislative regulations accordingly.

The development process of welfare state can be handled by categorizing in three periods. The first period was between 1870 and 1913, in other words from the late seventeenth century when the industrial revolution took place to early nineteenth century. The next period was the time between World War I and World War II and the time period between 1950 and 1973 when is referred to as the "Golden Age of Welfare States." Welfare state changed with the economic crises which realized after 1973. This period is referred to as "Welfare State Crisis" and refers to the period up today.

The emergence of welfare state dates back to 1601, when Poor Laws were put in force in UK. In this period, most of men were recruited for war. When they turned back home, they lived the rest of their life without any social security or protection but under risks. 1601 Poor Law was the first legislative initiative to protect the elders, patients, and wounded people in the society. However, this legislative regulation was not sufficient because the rest of society was also in need of protection. Another legislative regulation was made in 1834 as a result of economic and social pressure and because of the developments at the time. This is the beginning of the stigmatizing effects of social policy. In the following periods, the effects of Adam Smith's free market economy started to change the state policies and legislative regulations not only in UK but also in other countries.

Welfare state really emerged after World War II. Along World War I, all countries spent all of their resources for war. After World War I, it was understood that John Maynard Keynes approach was not sufficient for creating job opportunities and reviving public economy. After the war, it was believed that a second war could be prevented by means of creating job opportunities and providing new working and life standards.

With 1942 Social Security report (Social Insurance and Allied Services), Lord William Beveridge aimed at creating a health system, providing minimum income and decreasing employment rates. After the war, Beveridge's opinions were evaluated together with Keynes approach for creating a national welfare for UK [20]. Distrustfulness of liberalism urged countries for plunging into new quests.

States faced new social risks between 1870 and 1913. These risks were increase of aging population, pension payments, diseases, occupational diseases, and accidents. In 1880s, Bismarck made some efforts in order to provide social security. Reform efforts made by Bismarck aimed at providing a protection through social security against the risks of industrial revolution, low income, and population movements. The long working hours and heavy working conditions increased poverty and socialist movements. With these developments, the regulations covering disease insurance in 1883, work accident insurance in 1884, and old-age and disability insurance in 1889 were put in force.

Bismarck's reform movement aimed at establishing a system not only under the state but also with support of employers and employees. According to this, the system had three dimensions: employer's responsibilities, individual investments, and private insurance. This system also accepted the intervention by state. Therefore, it possible to say that the economic and political structures and, consequently, social policies of other countries started the change after Bismarck's reform.

Following Bismarck's reform, many legislative regulations were put in force for the diseases and injuries caused by industrialization. No similar regulations and rules had been put in force in Western European Countries until 1913.

Because of industrialization, the changes in social demographic structure, and increasing pressures in nineteenth century in European states, the realization of welfare state gained speed. Public sector and economy had a rapid development in China, Brazil, and Russia. Between 1950 and 1973, when it is known as the golden age of welfare state, the intervention of state gradually increased with the Keynesian approach which was adopted for solving the problems caused by the free market economy. However, Keynesian policies caused states to go into crises after 1970s. High tax rates, increasing public expenditures, and states' intervening markets were cited as the reasons for the crisis. In this period, when the proportion of social expenditures to public expenditures was gradually increasing, old-age, motherhood, injury, and death insurances were accepted in many countries. In addition, unemployment insurance and family aids were also regulated in more developed countries [21].

The welfare state has been undergoing a transformation since 1975. The state intervention which increased with 1929 economic crisis was replaced with a system in which the state shrined after the oil crisis between 1973 and 1979. In this period, states adopted the opinion that states should be less interventionist with regard to making economic and social policies. It is observed that the budget deficit which was caused by the pressure of social expenditures increased in this period when unemployment became chronic, inflation rate increased, and economic growth decreased especially in Western European countries.

Neoliberal approach which emerged in this period was adopted as a new form of liberalism, a result of solution seeking against Keynesian policies [22]. As a result of fierce competition caused by economic crises, a new period started in late 1970s, and in that period, Keynesian welfare state went through a crisis.

With globalization, welfare state that had stability in economic growth as well as good work conditions and price offers ended, and a new period in which nation states had less authority started. These developments which also affected social policies led to adoption of neoliberal approach for decreasing social expenditures. States started restructuring and new reforms in order to re-start economic growth. In the last 20 years, many countries have made regulations to decrease social expenditures. Yet again, in many countries, public expenditures have not decreased, instead, they have increased. The reasons of this condition are not only economic reasons and developments but also the reasons caused by the change of demographic structure like aging population and the changing family structure. As mentioned above, economic policies and social policies have mutual interactions. It is obvious that the changes in economic policies also affect social policies, and no one is independent of the other.

On the other hand, the economic condition of welfare state is not only related with individual behaviors but also related with social security system to be accepted for labor market and social welfare. The contradiction between labor market and state intervention has yet to be solved [17].

Welfare state continues to develop. State still plays an important role in determining social policies. It is possible to say that not only economic indicators but also the changes taking place in demographic and social structure play role in determining the policies of welfare state.

The welfare state aims at redistributing income and thus plays an interventionist and regulatory role. It takes measures to eliminate negativity in working life. It determines the minimum wage, undertakes social security and welfare services, and intervenes by taxes and other expenditures to eliminate injustices in income distribution [23, 24].

The welfare state is expressed as the deepened and extension of the classic protective state [25]. The welfare state, whose last stage reached has been by the modern state, is no longer a "spectator state," but it is a "player state" [19].

All of the definitions regarding welfare state include the mentality to protect those who have poor economic and social conditions. This protection can be done through social policies. Therefore, welfare state's intervention for the sake of eliminating the negative conditions, which is required to be done by the welfare state and achieve the goals of social policies, is appropriate and required.

Although the duties and scope of each welfare state change based on each country's social, cultural, economic and demographic conditions; basically, they include ensuring the protection of children, the disabled, families, the elders and women, creating jobs, providing education and vocational training, struggling against poverty and low income, and improving the working conditions.

Considering the practices of the welfare state, various distinctions have been made on the basis of services and expenditures to ensure social welfare. The most important study about this issue has been made by Gosta Esping-Andersen. Esping-Andersen classifies welfare state systems as follows:

- Liberal welfare model which is practiced by USA and UK
- Conservative and Continental Europe model which is practiced by Germany, France, and Belgium
- Social Democratic Scandivian Model which is practiced by Sweden and Denmark [26, 27].

The welfare state, emerging as a response to the search for solutions to address the inequalities and negativities created by the industrial revolution, is a new form of the liberal state. Because the liberal approach threatening social interests due to the fact that capital and markets were not interfered and the socialist approach that kept the interests of the working class at the highest level were not sufficient to meet the social needs, the welfare state emerged as a system to overcome the problems of both of these systems.

Regarding the welfare state, it is possible to make the following determinations regarding the period until the beginning of the process of globalization and neoliberalism [28].

- The residual approach evolved and replaced by with an institutional approach.
- Demanding social welfare has turned into a human right arising from being a citizen.
- While it was an understanding of service to meet the needs of only poor, it has turned into universal service to meet the needs of the whole society.
- It left from a limited welfare budge to large welfare expenditures.
- The understanding that such problems as poverty and unemployment are not because of the mistakes done by individuals but because of inadequacy of the state and its institutions.
- Making efforts to take responsibility for providing social welfare has shifted from volunteer individuals and institutions to public institutions.

The economic crises experienced after the 1970s caused problems and criticized the Keynesian welfare state. Budget deficit was one of the problems that were faced due to the increase in unemployment, the decrease in economic growth, and the increase in retirement age and health expenditures due to the aging of the population. The criticism and debate about the welfare state are that all the negative, economic, social, and political problems are caused by the social policy practices of the welfare state.

Long-term consideration of demographic changes and the impact of globalization on the welfare state have opened new avenues for debate and discussion about the welfare state's future development [17]. The important point is providing people welfare for the welfare states.

Criticisms about the welfare state are:

- Poverty and unemployment rates have not been reduced, and social welfare policies have not been successful

- The opportunities provided for welfare cause negative effects on family structure, increase divorce rates, and deteriorate moral values

- It has increased the taxes put on income and capital

- Social expenditures have increased [28, 29].

Welfare states have begun to develop new policies and restructure due to the problems that constitute the source of criticisms of social policy. Although it is claimed that the welfare state has a tendency to go back due to economic and financial pressures, it is possible to say that the welfare state continues to make efforts to adapt with the new conditions.

3.2 Globalization

The transformations which have taken place in social policy and welfare state can be explained under the shade of globalization. In 1998s and 1990s, privatization and marketization had an impact for some of conservative governments. The governments had more liberal approach to civil society and economy policy.

Globalization reveals a free market economy, liberal democracy, and cultural differences in the process leading to a holistic world economy [30]. Globalization process gained momentum after 1980. In this process which was based on economic liberalization, the neoliberal model became dominant and the idea that state should abandon its active role in social policies was adopted. In some developed countries, which had been practicing the neoliberal model, social policy implementations began to lose their importance, and they were completely neglected in less developed countries.

The effects of globalization became more evident at the end of the twentieth century, and the welfare state had less intrusive character with regard to taking measures for social protection due to the pressure caused by social expenditures and increased taxes. With the adoption of the dominant view that social expenditures hampered economic growth, the shrinking of welfare states and reduction of its role on social policies gained momentum. Due to the increasing competition between the welfare states, poverty and unemployment have increased, and injustices have emerged in the distribution of income [21].

The narrowing of social welfare state practices in the process of globalization caused social rights to be restricted. Liberal understanding limits the state's duties with the provision of security, justice, and infrastructure. State shrinks through liberalization. The possibility of the deterioration of the balance between capital and labor, which was tried to be established after the industrial revolution, threatens those who are in need of social protection. The increasing unemployment rate is one of the most important threats.

In the process of globalization, contrary to their liberal philosophy, the states that turned into neoliberal models needed to further develop their social policy practices. Developments show that, contrary to expectations, the model adopted in the process of globalization deepens the problems of social policies further.

The impacts of globalization on the welfare state model and social policies are evaluated from four different perspectives, which are:

- According to Mishra; globalization eliminates the independence of nation states. Economic growth is the sole target. International wage inequality and poverty increase due to economic pressures, and social protection is weakening. Welfare of nation states decreases with neoliberal policies [31].

- According to Pierson, globalization alone is not the reason for the reduction of the power of welfare states. As an external power, globalization may require renewal in the structuring of states, but this restructuring should not be a reduction of social policies. In this process, states should also take into account the internal effects such as demographic, migration, and social developments and decide on the restructuring process accordingly [32].

- According to Esping-Anderson, nation states should prefer more balanced practices on the axis of globalization. Nation states with strong economic and political structures should prefer the most harmonious practices for their own future while guiding globalization [27].

- According to Rieger and Leibfried, globalization emerged as a result of efforts of the nation states to reduce the negative effects of war with the liberal model. The economies of nation states are independent of the global economy; therefore, the restructuring process and the establishment of relevant policies should be evaluated in this respect [33].

The causes of the crisis of the welfare state in developed countries are globalization which is an external factor and internal variables which are related to the social structures of states. One of these reasons is the demographic structure, which has changed because of the aging population, prolongation of life, and decreasing birth rates. In addition, family structure has changed, divorces have increased, public expenditures, pension and health expenditures, and taxes have increased, and economic growth has declined. The competitive power of the countries in the international arena has decreased due to the increase in the expenditures of the welfare state to ensure social welfare. Having been in search of providing solution for the elimination of the financial pressures caused by the expenditures related to increased welfare, the welfare states have entered into a restructuring process.

In the restructuring and surviving process, the financial pressure was tried to be eased through the privatization of the pension system, raising the retirement age, increasing the premiums, and reducing the financial pressure.

With the shrinkage in the welfare state, the provision of welfare services has also changed. The service provision which had been performed by the state has been given through local administrations at local level, and it has been left to the non-profit organization, which means it has been "privatized" [28].

4. Future of the welfare state and social policy

It seems hard to foresee the future state of welfare state clearly because of variables. Welfare state changes based on social, economic, cultural, and demographic structures of states. It does not seem possible to provide financing of welfare statement with traditional methods. Especially 2008 financial crisis, welfare state had a view that a system in which the main player is the state is not sufficient for economic growth. The increasing unemployment is an obstacle for the welfare state growth. Moreover, the population of many states is getting older, and the demographic structure is changing. Labor markets need to be supported, new jobs need to be created, and employment needs to be increased. Therefore, states determined their policies. Public expenditures are increasing due to increasing pension payments with the aging population.

The expectations that welfare state provides welfare are increasing more and more. The approaches for providing welfare are different. Some states adopt liberal approaches, some states adopt corporatist and some others adopt universal approaches. In recent years, the belief that economic policies are not sufficient for achieving a welfare state but that welfare state needs to be achieved through social policies has been increasing.

Although many arguments have been raised in discussions on the future of the welfare state, it is possible to say that the rightist and leftist views are more dominant.

- The rightists argue that the welfare state can overcome the crisis only by shifting to neoliberal policies. They also argue that the obligatory change that took place in the industrial revolution is also valid for the Information Age which emerged in the last quarter of the twentieth century and that social policies need to be developed by the supranational organizations after the change of welfare state.

- For the leftists, they argue that welfare states have the ability to adapt themselves changing conditions; and therefore, they can overcome the crisis through reforms and restructuring. It is suggested that the neo-Keynesian approaches should be adopted instead of the neoliberal approach in the reform process.

As an alternative to these views, neoliberals and conservatives have made new initiatives under the name of "New Right," and social democrats and social liberals have made new initiatives under the name "The Third Way" [21].

Furthermore, the legitimacy of the welfare state was questioned by both The New Right and The New Left. The New Left criticized the state's role was too weak compared to the markets, and a reformulation of the state's role in societal development was needed. The New Right is focused on the role of bureaucracy and pressure groups. According to their opinion, society's welfare is more important than bureaucracy and pressure groups' interests [17].

The globalization, which has been cited as a reason for the transformation of the welfare state and social policies, increases its influence with the participation of international organizations such as World Bank, World Health Organization, and International Monetary Fund [13, 34, 35]. Nation states should implement policies in economic and social spheres not based on external processes but based on internal dynamics. As stated above, although they have similar features, each country has different applications for social protection. Here, the main important thing is to determine the impacts of change on demographic and cultural structures of the countries and make intervention properly. In summary, it is the choice of national political authorities to present the effects of globalization as the only reason for their national policies. Instead of this perspective, it would be a more realistic approach to try to benefit from the positive impacts of globalization for reducing problems at the national level. By this way, it would be possible to develop more effective tools to prevent the increasing social problems.

Welfare states are still developing. States are in search for better work and life conditions. They want to have social security systems which cover all social risks. From this perspective, it is possible to say that there is not a real crisis in welfare states, but there are efforts to remove obstacles before the economic growth.

Welfare states need to make regulations to decrease unemployment rates, taxes, and public expenditures because of the decline in economic growth [17]. There seems to be a tendency for narrowing in social policies because the proportion of social expenditures in public expenditures is high.

Reform initiatives to reduce the welfare crises in the welfare states have led to giving more importance to "active social protection" understanding in social policy implementations [36]. These practices, which were put into practice in 1990s and which aimed to be active in the labor market, were based on regulations that encourage working and restricting passive expenditures. In order to reduce the passive expenditures, the period of benefiting from social benefits was shortened, and their conditions were made difficult. When the impact of the reform implementations on social expenditures is evaluated, it is seen that poverty of children has increased and the works for giving family aids and providing vocation education have been insufficient. It is obvious that retirement age and health expenditures will continue to increase due to the aging population. It is possible to say that the increase of passive expenditures due to the aging of the population constitutes an obstacle before realization of active and passive reforms [37].

As a result, welfare states continue to exist in different ways. The developments show that the view that social rights, freedoms, and ideological thoughts are not sufficient to achieve the economic growth. It is possible to say that the welfare states having this view will follow impartial policies about making social expenditures in future years.

5. Conclusions

In this study, the social policy and the welfare state are handled with their goals, scopes, types, and problems from their historical development up to today.

Social policy is a set of measures developed to protect workers against the dangers arising as a result of industrialization, in parallel to the historical development, after the industrial revolution. Its emergence in this way has caused the social policies to be defined in a narrow sense. After World War II, the narrow perspective on social policy began to change. The reason of this change was the fact that the measures to protect the interests of the working class were not sufficient to solve social problems. Therefore, it was concluded that social policy should be extended to cover all segments of society. In a broad sense, social policy is a set of measures taken to ensure that all segments of the society live in peace and harmony to prevent unemployment, to improve working conditions, to provide a minimum wage, to provide social security and benefits, to eliminate injustice in income distribution, and to ensure social justice. Social policy refers to all policies that ensure the welfare of the state and individuals and the dynamic practices that constantly change.

The main goal of social policies is to ensure that everyone in society lives in peace and harmony away from conflicts. With social policies, it is aimed to ensure social justice, social development, social balance, social integration, and social peace.

The goal of social justice is to create equality of opportunity for every individual without eliminating the freedoms and to ensure a fair distribution of income. In particular, objective of justice is to provide services such as education, tax, social security, equal opportunities, and fair and adequate wages. Providing social balance is possible by eliminating social and regional differences. For the establishment of social peace, the factors that hinder social reconciliation must be eliminated. The aim of social integration is to ensure that measures are taken to prevent social disintegration. Social democracy, which has been adopted as the main objective of social policy, refers to the protection of individuals' interests in the environment of democratic freedoms by taking into account the balance of equality.

The industrial revolution played an important role in the historical development of social policies. After the industrial revolution, the increased capital ensured the formation of a powerful and rich bourgeoisie. On the other hand, the need for manpower was met by means of the working class. The gap between these two segments in society gradually increased. With the power from capital, the bourgeoisie class began to impose low wages, poor working conditions, and working hours of up to 16–20 hours on workers. The working class was left totally unprotected with the adoption of a liberal approach which argues that interference with market conditions adversely affects welfare. The increasing social problems led to the formation of social policies. The liberal market economy, which was replaced with Keynesian policies after World War II and 1929 economic crisis, was given up, and thus, the state could interfere with market by means of social policies.

Although there are many definitions of the welfare state, it is possible to say "It is a kind of state in which consciously organized public power is used to reduce the role of market forces." Shifting from a liberal model to Keynesian model of welfare state, states adopted a more interventionist character from economic, social, and legal points of view. Dating back to 1880s, the welfare state continued to strengthen until the mid-1970s due to the increased unemployment and spread of poverty in all countries.

The concept of welfare state entered into literature with the Beveridge Report, which was created in 1942. Looking at the foundations of the concept of welfare state, it is possible to say that it dates back to social security practices introduced by Bismarck in 1883. Welfare state emerged first in Germany and then in Western Europe, North America, and Australia. The common feature of these countries was that they had industrialization and developed market economies and democratic systems. South Korea, Hong Kong, Singapore, and Taiwan, which underwent a further industrialization process, started to be accepted as welfare states in the 1970s. Japan had completed this process earlier. While there were attempts to become a welfare state in the Soviet Union after the Bolshevik Revolution in 1917, the efforts to become a welfare state began later in China, Cuba, and Eastern Europe but they did not achieve an accomplishment with this regard because they had no industrialization.

Social policy, which emerged as a result of failure of the social problems created by the liberal economy approach, was replaced with the concept of welfare state after the adoption of social security practices introduced by Bismarck in Germany.

The social state developed policies not only in the areas of health, education, social security, distribution of income, and housing but also sought solutions to environmental and urban problems in order to ensure social welfare. The welfare state varies from country to country according to the level of welfare they have. According to the classification made by Esping-Anderson, liberal welfare model belongs to conservative Continental Europe, while the social democratic model belongs to Scandinavians.

It is possible to say that the welfare state, which was developed to eliminate the deficiencies of the liberal and socialist understanding in welfare, is a new form of liberal model. In this sense, it acts with an interventionist approach to solve the problems that may arise in the field of social policy.

The Keynesian welfare state stated to have a tendency to narrow social expenditures due to the decrease of economic growth, unemployment, and increased budget deficits after the economic crises seen in the 1970s.

The criticism that the welfare state's practices for welfare were unsuccessful was justified based on allegations that poverty and unemployment increased, tax and social expenditures constituted a big burden, and the family and moral structure in the society changed unfavorably.

Welfare state's tendency to turn back retrogressively is most likely to have a negative impact on social policies. The financial pressures caused by social expenditures may cause the welfare state to take on a passive character as in the liberal period in the face of social problems and cause social policies to regress.

This retrogression in the welfare is justified with globalization process, which has started to show its effects since the late 1970s. The understanding of globalization which is accompanied by liberalization suggests the limitation of the duties of the state. This situation may cause deeper problems in the social field. Although globalization had an impact on the welfare state as an external factor, it is also necessary to evaluate the internal factors related to the socioeconomic and demographic structures of the states in the emergence of the crisis.

Demographic structure that changed because of the aging of the population, prolongation of life span, and decreasing birth rates can be shown as a reason for the crisis of the welfare state in developed countries. In addition, the family structure changed, public expenditures, pension and health expenditures, and taxes increased, and economic growth decreased. The competitive power of the welfare state decreased due to the increase in expenditures made to ensure social welfare. The welfare states, which are in search of a solution for the elimination of the financial pressures caused by the expenditures related to increased prosperity, have entered into a restructuring process. In the process of restructuring and surviving, the financial pressure was tried to be eased through the privatization of the retirement system, raising the retirement age, and increasing the premiums. During the restructuring process, the privatization initiatives were accelerated by providing the social welfare service through local administrations at local level.

There are many views on the future of the welfare state. Rightists who provide solutions to overcome the crisis argue that the neoliberal approach should be adopted, while leftists argue that neo-Keynesian approaches should be adopted.

In today's world, the concept of welfare state is transforming and the economic pressures created by globalization have a tendency to narrow social policies. Based on the fact that the reason for the transformation in the welfare state is not just globalization, each state should develop policies and tools that are the most appropriate for its social structure to adapt it to the transformation process. In fact, when we look at the practices of the welfare states in the world, it is possible to say that the effects of the crisis differ according to the level of development and welfare. Some of the welfare states continue to undertake initiatives to reduce public expenditures but they fail to satisfy the expectations especially because of the demographic structure. It is impossible to reduce the health and retirement expenditures because of the increasingly aging population.

The reform initiatives to reduce the crisis in the welfare states in the 1990s adopted the "active social protection" understanding, which aimed at activation by keeping the work force in labor market active in social policy practices. In order to reduce the passive expenditures, the period of benefiting from social benefits was shortened, and their conditions were made difficult. Considering OECD data, it is seen that the activation efforts fail short to satisfy the expectations. On the other hand, it is seen that family and care support are not provided enough, and child poverty increases. Activation of practices is implemented by many countries. It can be said that the time passed is not enough to give a decision whether the activation efforts have positive effects. However, it is clear that retirement and health expenditures will continue to increase due to the aging population.

Inflation, tax, and public expenditures need to be reduced in order that the welfare state continues its existence and economic growth and increases its competitiveness. In Europe, where there is tradition of social solidarity, there is a tendency that the welfare state continues. With the support of international organizations such as IMF, OECD, and World Bank, welfare states transfer the distribution of social services to the private sector. However, welfare services are still planned by the state, and many services are still provided by the state.

Despite all these developments, it is possible to say that the welfare state has an active role on social policies and welfare states are resistant to the economic negativities experienced. In our opinion, reducing social expenditures should be the last resort in the reform initiatives of states to achieve growth in the future periods of transformation of the welfare state. The strategies to be established in this way should be determined in light of the following points:

- Not deviating from the goal of achieving ultimate welfare in the transferring of services to the private sector and preserving the regulatory, descriptive character of the state

- Encouraging the private sector with regard to distribution of social services

- Making use of the increasing of voluntary organizations and local governments with regard to the provision of social services

- Restructuring to reduce expenditures other than social assistance expenditures

- Attaching importance to giving child care money to families and importance to young people's vocational education, considering the obstacles caused by the demographic structure

- Reducing the burden of unemployment in public social spending by producing solutions that can prevent the increasing and deepening unemployment in the world

- Reducing the inflation and tax

- Not considering decreasing the spending on social welfare as a tool for economic growth and determining the economic strategies on this basis

- Utilizing the developments on a global scale in favor of the social welfare state and adopting strategies in line with the positive effects of globalization and making cooperation with international and supranational organizations in this process

In the light of all these points, it is possible to say that in the future, the governments adopting approaches compromising social policies in order to achieve economic growth will lead to the reaction of the society who has the expectation of social welfare. On the other hand, achieving welfare without deviating from the goals of social policy will also vary according to the states' ability to adapt themselves to changes and developments and reconstructing accordingly.

Author details

Esra Dundar Aravacik
Faculty of Economics and Administrative Sciences, Healthcare Institutions Management Department, Health Law, Izmir Katip Celebi University, Turkey

*Address all correspondence to: esra.dundar@ikc.edu.tr

References

[1] Ersöz HY. Sosyal Politikada Yerelleşme. Istanbul: ITO; 2011. p. 99

[2] Altan ÖZ. Sosyal Politika. Eskişehir: Anadolu Üniversitesi Yayını; 2009

[3] Erdal L. Türkiye'de Sosyal Politika ve Koruyucu Aile Hizmet Modeli. Sosyoekonomi. 2014;**22**:171-192. Available from: sosyoekonomi.dergipark.gov.tr/download/article-file/197793 [Accessed: 27-10-2018]

[4] Talas C. Türkiye'nin Açıklamalı Sosyal Politika Tarihi. Ankara: Bilgi Yayınevi; 1992

[5] Selçuk FÜ. Sosyal Politika: Tarihsel Zorunluluk Yaklaşımı Yerine Liberalizmle Ortaklaşan, Temellerden Alternatif Kurumsal İnşalara. Bilgi Dergisi. 2008;**2**:17

[6] Özaydın M. Küresel Etkilerle Şekillenen Sosyal Politika Anlayışı Ekseninde Sosyal Politikaların Geleceğini Tartışmak. Gazi Üniversitesi İktisadi ve İdari Bilimler Fakültesi Dergisi. 2008;**10**(1):163-180. Available From: http://iibfdergisi.gazi.edu.tr/index.php/iibfdergisi/article/view/123/114 [Accessed: 25-10-2018]

[7] Sami Güven H. Sosyal Politikanın Temelleri. 4th ed. Bursa: Ezgi Kitabevi; 2009. (online) Available from: http://0212n0ytd.y.http.eds.a.ebscohost.com.ikcu.proxy.deepknowledge.io/eds/ebookviewer/ebook?sid=9c85753d-8564-462c-8226-b50342ff6626%40sdc-v-sessmgr02&vid=0&format=EB [Accessed: 27-10-2018]

[8] Kleinman M. Crisis? What crisis? Contunity and change in European welfare states. In: Buğra DA, Keyder Ç, editors. Sosyal Politika yazıları. 2th ed. İstanbul: İletişim Yayınları; 2006

[9] Kennet P. Introduction: The changing context of comparative social policy. In: A Handbook of Comparative Social Policy. UK: Edward Elgar Publishing; 2004

[10] Livemore M, Midgley J. Handbook of Social Policy. 2th ed. USA: Sage Publication; 2009. Available from: http://0212n0yut.y.http.eds.a.ebscohost.com.ikcu.proxy.deepknowledge.io/eds/ebookviewer/ebook?sid=2ef1eef2-4415-4ecf-b727-5f174764d263%40sessionmgr4006&vid=0&format=EK [Accessed: 26-10-2018]

[11] Blakemore K, Warwick-Booth L. Social Policy, An Introduction. McGraw Hill, Ed. England: Open University Press; 2013. Available from: http://0212n0ytw.y.http.eds.a.ebscohost.com.ikcu.proxy.deepknowledge.io/eds/ebookviewer/ebook?sid=c7700036-22d7-4c6f-bbaf-b0272df89753%40sessionmgr4006&vid=0&format=EB [Accessed: 27-10-2018]

[12] Daly M. Governence and social policy. Journal of Social Policy. 2003;**32**(1):113-128. DOI: 10.1017/S0044727940200684O. Available from: http://www/Cambridge.org/core/terms [Accessed: 25-10-2018]

[13] Deacon B. Global Social Policy and Governance. London: Sage Publications; 2007

[14] Robinson A, Moggridge D. The Collected Writings of John Maynard Keynes: The General Theory of Employment, Interest and Money. 4th ed. Vol. 2013. Cambridge University Press. p. 7

[15] Erdut Z. Uluslararası Sosyal Politika ve Türkiye Küreselleşme Bağlamında. İzmir: DEU Yayınları; 2002

[16] Çubuk A. Sosyal Politika. Vol. 123. Ankara: İktisadi ve Ticari İlimler Akademisi Yay; 1979

[17] Greve B. Welfare State. 3th ed2014. Available from: http://0212n0ytl.y.http.eds.b.ebscohost.com.ikcu.proxy.deepknowledge.io/eds/ebookviewer/ebook?sid=bf 88060a-95ec-4185-b6c0-38ee92569537%40pdc-v-sessmgr03&vid=0&format=EK [Accessed: 26-10-2018]

[18] Asa B. The welfare state at historical perspective. Archives européennes de sociologie. 1961;**2**(2):221-259. Available from: https://ikcu.proxy.deepknowledge.io/MuseSessionID=021010ytv/MuseProtocol=https/MuseHost=www.jstor.org/MusePath/stable/23987939?https://ikcu.proxy.deepknowledge.io/MuseSessionID=021010ytv/MuseProtocol=https/MuseHost=www.jstor.org/MusePath/stable/23987939&seq=1#metadata_info_tab_contents [Accessed: 28-10-2018]

[19] Serter N. Devlet Görevlerindeki Gelişmelerin Sonucu Olarak Sosyal Devlet. İstanbul: İstanbul Üniversitesi IIBF Yayını; 1994

[20] Rodgers B. Towards a Welfare State. 2014. Available from: http://0212n0yts.y.http.eds.a.ebscohost.com.ikcu.proxy.deepknowledge.io/eds/ebookviewer/ebook?sid=73c12b83-c3ad-40a6-aec5-69a1aca9dc62%40sessionmgr4007&vid=0&format=EK [Accessed: 28-10-2018]

[21] Özdemir S. Küreselleşme Sürecinde Refah Devleti. 2th ed. İstanbul Ticaret Odası Yayını; 2007. p. 57. Available from: http://0212n0yue.y.http.eds.a.ebscohost.com.ikcu.proxy.deepknowledge.io/eds/ebookviewer/ebook?sid=9fd54384-c96d-420e-9163-a37f9cb5a810%40sessionmgr4010&vid=0&format=EB [Accessed: 26-10-2018]

[22] Şenkal A. Küreselleşme Sürecinde Sosyal Politika. İstanbul: Alfa Yayınları; 2005

[23] Clarke J, Hughes G, Lewis G, Money G. Introduction: The Meaning of the Welfare State, Social Policy: Welfare, Power and Diversity (Imagging Welfare Futures). New York: Open University Press; 1998

[24] TUSIAD. Optimal Devlet. Istanbul: Tusiad Yayınları; 1995

[25] Rosanvallon P. Refah Devletinin Krizi, Çev. B. Şahinli, Ankara: Dost Kitabevi; 2004

[26] Esping-Anderson G. The Three World of Welfare Capitalism. Oxford: Polity Press; 1990

[27] Anderson E. Social Foundations of Postindustrial Economics. New York: Oxford University Press; 1999

[28] Özdemir S. Küreselleşme Sürecinde Refah Devleti. Vol. 69. İstanbul: İstanbul Ticaret Odası Yayınları; 2004

[29] Glazer N. The Limits of Social Policy. Cambridge: Harvard University Press; 1990. Available from: https://www.jstor.org/stable/1289340. DOI: 10.2307/1289340

[30] Aktel M. Küreselleşme Süreci ve Etki Alanları. Süleyman Demirel Üniversitesi İktisadi ve İdari Bilimler Fakültesi Dergisi. 2001;**6**(2):193-202. Available from: http://021300ytf.y.http.dergipark.gov.tr.ikcu.proxy.deepknowledge.io/download/article-file/195121 [Accessed: 28-10-2018]

[31] Mishra R. Globalization and the Welfare State. UK: Edward Elgar Publishing; 1999

[32] Pierson C. Beyond the Welfare State? The New Economy of Welfare. Cambridge: Cambridge Polity Press; 2006

[33] Reiger E, Leibfried S. Limits to Globalization: Welfare States and the World Economy. UK: Blackwell; 2003

[34] Yeates N. Globalization and social policy. From global neoliberal

hegemony to global political plurism. Global Social Policy. 2001;**2**(1):69-91, Sage Publications, London, Available from: http://journals.sagepub.com/doi/pdf/10.1177/1468018102002001095 [Accessed: 26-10-2018]

[35] Holden C. Global social policy: An application of welfare state theory. Journal of International and Comparative Social Policy. 2017;**34**(1):40-57. Available from: https://0211r0yu9-y-https-www-tandfonline.com.ikcu.proxy.deepknowledge.io/doi/full/10.1080/21699763.2017.1413993?scroll=top&needAccess=true [Accessed: 27-10-2018]

[36] Palier B. The re-orientation of European social policies towards social investment. International Journal of Politics, Culture, and Society. 2006:105-116. Available from: https://hal-sciencespo.archives-ouvertes.fr/hal01020968/document [Accessed: 29-10-2018]

[37] OECD Statistics. Available from: https://stats.oecd.org/viewhtml.aspx?datasetcode=PAG&lang=en, https://stats.oecd.org/viewhtml.aspx?datasetcode=WEALTH&lang=en, https://stats.oecd.org/viewhtml.aspx?datasetcode=FAMILY&lang=en, https://stats.oecd.org/viewhtml.aspx?datasetcode=IDD&lang=en [Accessed: 27-10-2018]

Chapter 2

Theory of Public Debt and Current Reflections

Sibel Aybarç

*"The public debt is a burden on the back of our children and grandchildren...
All debt is evil; public debt absolutely evil* [1]."

Abstract

From the ancient ages to today, administrations needed continuous financing and met this financing with various sources. The process of social development necessitated public borrowing for different purposes ranging from *creation of a consumer society to sell the surplus of developed countries* to *postwar human relations* and from the *development financing of developing countries* to the *payment of debt by debt*. Particularly after World War II (1941–1945), the developed countries provided the external resources to developing countries for development financing. As a result of the increase in the mobility of capital in the process of globalization (especially short-term speculative capital investments), developing countries were dragged to the debt-interest helix problem and the external debt crises. The stabilization programs proposed by the IMF led to government guarantee of private sector external debts in the developing countries and led to a rapid increase in the public debt stock.

Keywords: public debt, internal debt, external debt, crowding out, globalization

1. Definition of public debts

In the modern state perspective, the needs constantly increase; therefore, the state has to spend more to meet these needs. Public expenditures are generally met by ordinary public revenues such as taxes, duties, fees, parafiscal revenues, property and enterprise revenues, taxes, and penalties. However, the state is faced with the public sector deficit due to reasons such as large infrastructure investments, war, development financing, natural disasters, economic crises, budget deficits, as well as the ever-increasing ordinary public expenditures. To overcome this situation, they refer to borrowing.

Borrowing is the taking of money and similar values for repayment after a certain period of time. Public borrowing refers to the legal obligation of the state to pay back the principal and interest to the holders of the predetermined rights in accordance with a certain schedule. Public credit and public borrowing referred as state borrowing in the economic literature mean debts taken by government or other public institutions [2].

Governments in ancient and medieval ages required funding, as in modern states. But governments did not borrow "publically" in the concept of drawing funds from a large populace and paying principal and interest, as like deferred taxes [3].

In the thirteenth century, public borrowing, including even the king's borrowing, was first scientifically examined by Charles Davemont in 1710. Thereafter, economists such as David Hume, Adam Smith, D. Ricardo, Malthus, J.S. Mill, J.B. Say, A.P. Lerner, and A.G. Hart have worked on borrowing. Smith and Ricardo opposed public borrowing. In their view, borrowing can be spent irresponsibly because of being an easy income; so that causes deterioration in the functioning of economic life. In this context, the classics have advocated that capital is wasted, and the debt burden is transferred to the next generations due to the inefficiency of public expenditures [4]. In addition, classics have defended that borrowing could be in some case such as large infrastructure investment and war but emphasized that it should be limited and not be kept on.

The public borrowing policies over the world have especially experienced a turning point with the World War I (1914–1918) and the Great Depression (1930s). During the period in question, John Maynard Keynes had proposed public borrowing as a war financing to England and argued that it would be useful. In the process that started with this proposal, public borrowing became an indispensable source of financing for the states. This situation does not mean that states participated in Keynesian theory. While public borrowing becomes an indispensable source of financing, it also brings the debt-interest cycle, poverty, and crises. The result of public borrowing leaves a great burden on the next generations. This situation has justified the classics [4].

Especially after the World War II, public borrowing indicated both significant increase and structural changes due to on the one hand the repair works of the countries affected by the war, on the other hand, the financing needs of developing countries [5]. In the following period, the borrowing process are no longer interstate and have started to gain a new dimension by establishing international organizations such as International Monetary Fund (IMF), World Bank (WB), International Finance Corporation (IFC), International Development Association (IDA), European Investment Bank (EIB), and Islamic Development Bank (IDB).

In the process of globalization, the mobility of capital has increased; and serious financial competition has emerged in global markets.

In particular, developing countries have sought to use them to development financing by attracting international short-term capital movements to their countries through various incentive instruments (such as low taxes, high interest rates, etc.). However, both the sudden fluctuation in capital movements and the implemented incentive mechanisms have dragged the developing countries to the external debt spiral.

2. Classification of public debts

Public debts are classified into various types according to their characteristics. When the public debt literature is analyzed, it is classified into three main groups according to maturity, resources, and voluntariness [6–9] (**Figure 1**):

- Public debts according to maturities: short-, medium-, and long-term public debts
    - *Short-term public debts (floating debts)* refer to debts up to 1 year. In short-term borrowing, treasury bills and treasury guaranteed bond are used.
    - *Medium-term public debts* refer to debts ranging from 1 to 5 years.
    - *Long-term public debts refer* to debts more than 5 years. The instrument of long-term borrowing is the government bond. These debts are provided from

the capital markets and have a higher interest rate than the interest rate of short-term borrowing. Long-term debts are classified as redeemable debts and irredeemable debts.

- Public debts according to sources: internal debts and external debts
    - *Internal borrowing* refers to a country's borrowing from own national resources. This borrowing has no effect on increasing or decreasing national income.
    - *External borrowing* refers to the resources provided from a foreign country that is repaid with principal and interest at the end of a certain period. External debt has an increasing effect on national income when it is taken and vice versa has a decreasing effect on national income when it is paid.
- Public debt as a voluntary basis: voluntary debts and obligatory debts
    - *Voluntary debts* refer the debts that are lent to the state by its own will and desire.
    - *Obligatory debts* refer to the debts which are lent by forcing to take the bonds issued by the government. These debts are applied in times of war, natural disaster, or economic crises. In itself, it is classified as the debts taken by full compulsion, the debts taken by the threat of forcing, the debts taken by creating the necessary savings, and the liabilities taken by the moral coercion.

Productive and unproductive debts are also available. If the debts are used in construction, such as railways, power stations, and irrigation projects, which contribute to the productive capacity of the economy, they denote to productive debts. By this way, productive debts provide a constant flow of income to the state. The state generally pays the interest and principal debt amount from these projects' revenues. If the debts are used in the area such as war, famine relief, social services, etc., which do not contribute to the productive capacity of economy, they denote to unproductive debts. The state generally pays the interest and principal debt amount from taxes; therefore, these debts are a burden on the society [10–12] (**Figure 1**).

Today, rapidly increasing international relations have increased the importance of external debts. The less developed and developing countries have to refer to external borrowing for the realization of their economic development. The lack of adequate capital markets for development in these countries and the insufficient number of technical materials and personnel required external resources. As a matter of fact, these are the main reasons for applying to external borrowing in the Ottoman Empire and the Turkish Republic periods before internal borrowing [13].

Internal and external borrowing amounts are adversely progressed in less developed and developed countries. According to this, the debts of developed countries are predominantly internal debts; the debts of less developed and developing countries are mostly external debts. Because in developed countries, the state can easily provide the debts needed by own internal sources. It is also important from where and how the sources of funding are provided in a country's economy as well as how these resources are channeled back into the economy [13].

As it is known, external borrowing has an increasing effect on national income when taken and has a decreasing effect on national income when paid. Because of these features, it is important to use for what purpose external borrowing. For instance, the *development credits*, that are provided in order to investing in economic development and increasing the existing investments, contribute to the economy by using the programs and projects included in the development plans. Development credits are dealt within four groups [6, 9, 13]:

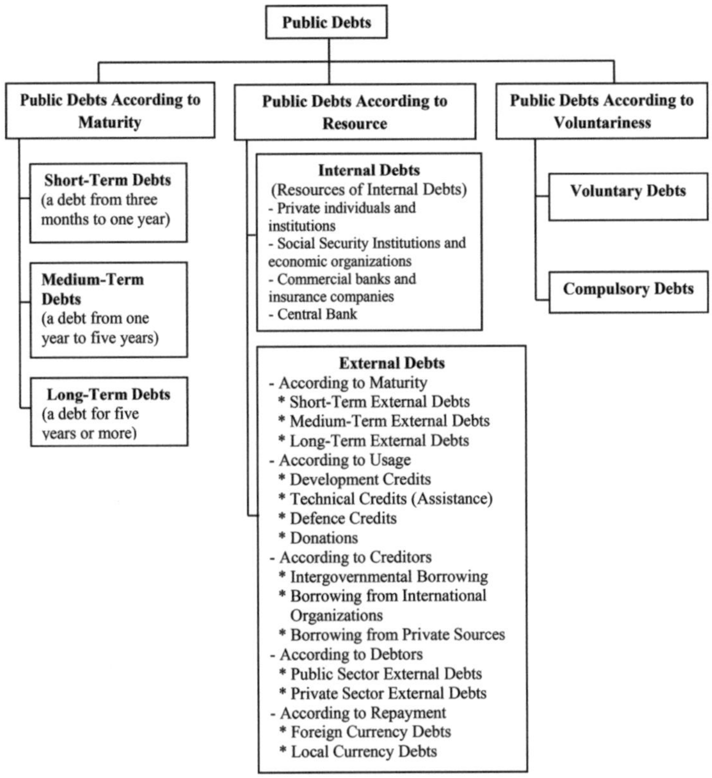

Figure 1.
Classification of public debts. Note: Prepared by the author by utilizing from literature.

- Project credits and program credits
  - *Project credits* are the credits that provided for the purpose of realizing the investment projects in the development plans of the countries. Countries that request credit provide projects with detailed information to countries or organizations that will give credit. Project credits are accredited/opened for the financing of eligible projects. Thus, less developed and developing countries are forced to use credits in a productive area, while creditor countries or organizations have the opportunity to control their credits. The biggest drawback of these credits is the long time for the preparation, submission, and creditor approval of the project, which makes the efficient use of credits more difficult.
  - *Program credits* are the credits that received for the purpose of importation of raw materials, semifinished goods, finished goods, and spare parts required for development targets in general. It is more flexible to use because it is not connected to any project. Thus, with the help of program credits, import bottlenecks are eliminated and the economy is kept in working condition. Therefore, it is a credit that is demanded more by developing countries.
- Tied loans and soft loans
  - *Tied loans* refer to the credit that should be used in the country which gave the credit. In this case, the debtor country does not have the authority to spend the credit on its own request. Nowadays this feature of loans granted

by developed countries generates to establish the system that is working in favor of the lender countries. Thus, the creditor country has provided advantages such as new foreign market, export growth, employment increase, and technology transfer. In terms of the debtor country, the situation is not bright at all. The borrower country is exposed to practices that increase the real cost of a loan such as buying a product from creditors at a much more expensive price than the normal market rate, transporting the goods through the creditor country's transport system and insuring them by the creditor country's insurance system. Hence, countries that receive loans remain under heavy debt burden.

- *Soft loans* are credits that granted the free use of developing countries. Thus, the debtor countries can provide the goods and services necessary for development financing from the international market in the cheapest way.

- Debt postponement and refinancing credits
  - *Debt postponement* is to postpone debt payment for an expired credit to a later date in return for a lower rate of interest compared to the first interest rate.
  - *Refinancing credits* are to pay an expired debt by the creditor country with the same amount of a new loan (a new debt). The main reason for creditor countries to accept debt postponement and refinancing credits is to enable them to accept some new commitments to the debtor country with these instruments. Thus, the creditor country can direct the debtor country's economic policies in line with its own advantages.

3. Effects of public debts

Borrowing has an important place among the public revenues, so its political, economic, and social impacts have great importance. The political effects of public borrowing are handled within the framework of political business cycle theory. According to theory, public expenditures increase during the election period. The government with the vote worry increases the public investments, but prefer to finance these public expenditures with internal borrowing instead of tax or emissions. In the short and medium term, governments, that do not want to seem repellent for voters, transfer the debt principal and interest payments to the next governments in the long term. This situation brings along the debt burden, which is often worsening with an alternative to closing debt with debt in developing countries [15].

Economic and social effects of borrowing take place in different ways in the following condition [4, 8]:

- To be long- or short-term maturity
- To spend or to keep the source that provided from borrowing
- To borrow from internal and external sources

The long-term or short-term maturity of public borrowing determines the duration of the contraction or expansionary effects. In this respect, the short-term borrowing changes the economic conjuncture frequently, because of the more liquidity and monetization feature of short-term debt instruments. If the resources obtained by borrowing are expended, it causes an expansionary effect; if the resources obtained by borrowing are not expended, it causes a contractionary effect [4].

In order to provide the expected results of debt policies (i.e., borrowing methods, credit instruments, and payment and redemption methods), the economic effects of borrowing should be well known and analyzed. At this point, the source of the public debt and the place where it is used gain importance [2, 4, 5, 8, 14, 16]:

- The effect of public debt on the general level of prices: It is true that borrowing will create a deflationary effect only when it is considered as a bond sale. Because the private sector uses its own resources for buying public bonds, therefore, the private demand and the total demand are decreasing. This situation causes deflation by reducing the general level of prices. However, the state purchases goods and services with the resources that are collected from the sale of bonds or bills; thus the total demand increases due to public demand. This situation causes inflation by increasing the general level of prices as a result of the operation of various mechanisms.

- The effect of public debt on income distribution: The effect of public debt on income distribution depends on which income groups burden with debt costs and depends on which income groups are the obtained debt sources transferred to. This effect usually occurs during the principal and interest repayments. In particular in the internal borrowing, if the taxpayers and the lenders to the government are the same person or organization, there will be no inequality in the income distribution. However, vice versa, if the principal and interest payments related to public debt are paid by taxes collected from the middle- to low-income groups, then there is a transfer of resources from the middle- and low-income groups to the high-income group. This situation causes income distribution, the detriment of the middle- and low-income group, to deteriorate. In terms of external borrowing, the income distribution to favor of those beneficiaries from public expenditures in the period which they were taken was effected by the external debts positively. On the other hand, the external borrowing will affect the income distribution for next generation due to the debt burden adversely (such as the reduction of public expenditures and excessive tax payment). The effect of public debts on income distribution also points to the social impact of public borrowing.

- The effect of public debts on savings volume and investments: As long as the government canalizes to investing the savings that are collected by the way of internal borrowing, national income will increase, and personal income and personal savings tendency will increase. If the government transfers to budget deficit or consumption of the resources which recollected by internal borrowing, it will reduce the private sector investment amount by affecting the private sector's total savings volume. This event is called crowding out. The slowdown of national income growth as a result of the decrease in investments shows the real burden of the financing with borrowing instead of tax on the next generation. When debt is used to finance public expenditure, its real cost to society is the sacrifice in private sector production [17].

- The effect of public debts on economic development: if the funds provided through borrowing for economic development can be canalized to infrastructure investments (such as dams, roads, ports, mining, agriculture), they increase the new investments through multiplier effect. As a result, national income and employment increase; and accordingly economic development is ensured. Nowadays, less developed and developing countries, which make the development effort, resort to external borrowing due to insufficient internal financing sources. If the aforementioned countries do not use external financing sources in the required fields, this situation may turn into debt financing by debt. This situation also shows the importance of debt management.

4. Current reflections of public debts

The phenomenon of globalization, which extends to geographical discoveries by origin, has gained momentum with the process of commercial and financial liberalization in the last quarter of the twentieth century. In this process, the globalization of capital, in particular, has dragged the developing countries, which have entered into a growth effort based on foreign capital, to the competition of encouragement (with high real interest rates, low exchange rates, and low tax rates). Increasing tax competition among developing countries led to a decrease in tax rates. The inadequate tax revenues for the financing of the increased public expenditures in these countries brought the need for new borrowing for the agenda. The application of high real interest rates to pay new debt principal and interest led to a rapid rise in the borrowing costs of developing countries and consequently a vicious cycle of debt-interest. Thus, the external borrowing process that developing countries started to finance development has undergone structural change. In this process, the method of closing the old debt with new debt (Ponzi-type financing) was adopted [18] (**Figure 2**).

Developing countries, which cannot overcome the lack of resources, have faced severe crises due to their fragile market structures. While the crises experienced until the 1980s stemmed from the balance of payment problems, in the globalization process, the nature of the crises has changed and has become the external debt crises and financial market crises (1982 Mexico, 1992–1993 ERM, 1994 Mexico, 1997 Asia, 1998 Russia, 1999 Brazil, 2000–2001 Turkey and Argentina) [19]. Thus, the volume of financial transactions in the global economy was only 15.3 times larger than the nominal GDP in the 1990s, while in the 2000s, it was 73.5 times larger. Equities, bonds, and foreign exchange spot transactions have nearly doubled the nominal GDP worldwide [20].

The world debt crises, which began with the declaration of the moratorium by Mexico in 1982 and spread by domino effect, caused the creditors to halt the supply of credit in a panic. Thus, developing countries, whose external debt burden has become more severe, had to implement the stabilization policies proposed by the IMF in order to get new loans or to delay debt. The process followed brought with

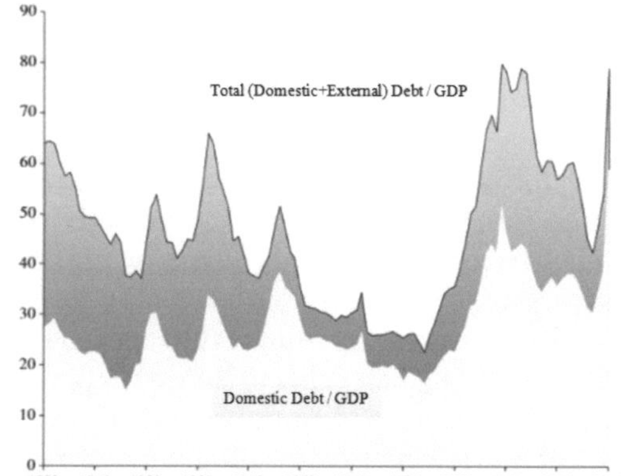

Figure 2.
Public debt (total and domestic debt) of all economies, as a percentage of GDP 1900–2010 [21].

inequalities in income distribution, unemployment, inflation, and poverty. On the other hand, developed countries have faced the problem of slowing capital accumulation due to the decrease in profit rates since the 1970s. This stagnation in developed countries has been tried to be overcome by lending excessive credit to developing countries through credit mechanism. Thus, both idle funds were evaluated in developed countries, and new markets were found for export increase [18].

For developed countries to sell the surplus production, firstly, it was necessary to create a consumer society. This is only possible by changing the basic habits of society. Intangible concepts such as cultural values, traditions, beliefs, etc. have gained importance as the basis for the use of the method of power based on economic power. Developed countries consciously use these power tools and encourage other countries to have their own culture and economic structure. In this way, it can be said that especially the developing countries are transformed into a consumer society, and thus they are continuously indebted for both public and private sectors [22].

In the globalization process, when the total external debt stock of developing countries is analyzed, it can be seen as a notable increase in short-term external debts and private sector external debts. Therefore, the process is called the rapid privatization of external debts. This phenomenon brings the important problems for developing countries. Short-term debts, which are not paid by the private sector (especially commercial banks) in times of crises, are taken under the state guarantee by IMF regulations. In the end, the short-term private sector debt was turned into long-term public debt by consolidating. After the 2001 crises in Turkey, we can see that the debt burden of bankrupt banks had transferred to the Treasury. As a result, Turkey's public debt has increased rapidly [18].

5. Conclusions

The state faced a financing deficit, when the ever-increasing needs in the social development process were not met by the state's ordinary public revenues (such as taxes, duties, fees, parafiscal revenues, property and enterprise revenues, taxes, and penalties). In addition to these expenditures, the state had to resort to borrowing due to major infrastructure investments, war, development financing, natural disasters, economic crisis, and budget deficits. From the borrowing of the king representing the country in the thirteenth century to the current debt crises, public borrowing has served different purposes in this process. This process has brought different debt types according to maturities (short, medium, long term), resources (internal and external debts), and voluntariness (voluntary and compulsory debts). Thus, borrowing overreached to be an extraordinary public revenue and has started to be perceived as a means of intervention to the economy. For example, the state uses internal debts as a tool to reduce demand in inflationary periods and to increase demand in deflationary periods.

In this section, which focuses on the political, economic, and social impacts and current reflections of borrowing in the context of public debt theory, the transformation in the external debt structure in the globalization process is emphasized. Initially external assistance and debts taken by developing countries as development financing have been used as a means to eliminate the stagnation by the developed countries in their economies. The given debts to the developing countries were used to increase the exports of developed countries, especially through tied loans. This situation has brought the new market, technology transfer, and economic power to the developed countries, while it has caused consumption society, external dependency, debt-interest spiral, and ultimately external debt crises in the developing countries. The restrictions of the structural adjustment programs have been introduced by IMF to improve the fragile economies of developing countries against external debt crises. In this period, IMF has started to use this structural adjustment programs, which include strict structural reforms, by determining the economic and social policies of the debtor countries as a tool to serve the purpose of developed countries.

Author details

Sibel Aybarç
Public Finance, Faculty of Economics and Administrative Sciences, Manisa Celal Bayar University, Turkey

*Address all correspondence to: sibel.aybarc@cbu.edu.tr

References

[1] Samuelson PA. Economics: An Introductory Analysis. 10th rev ed. USA: McGraw-Hill Inc.; 1976. p. 896. ISBN-10: 0070856419. ISBN-13: 978-0070856417

[2] Ulusoy A. Devlet Borçlanması. Trabzon: Aksakal Press; 2013. p. 358. ISBN: 975-98986-1-6

[3] Salsman RM. The Political Economy of Public Debt Three Centuries of Theory and Evidence, New Thinking in Political Economy Series. UK: Edward Elgar Publishing Limited; 2017. p. 336. ISBN-10: 1785363379

[4] Sugözü Hİ. Devlet Borçları IMF-Dünya Bankası ve Türkiye. Ankara: Nobel Press; 2010. p. 384. ISBN: 978-605-395-383-8

[5] Yaşa M. Devlet Borçları. Ankara: Ankara University Law Faculty Press; No: 421; 1978. p. 87

[6] Açba S. Devlet Borçlanması. Afyon: Pınar Press; 1994. p. 246

[7] Corina CR. Public Debt: Structure and Characteristics Romania's Case. Annals of the "Constantin Brâncuşi" University of Târgu Jiu. Economy Series. 2013;**3**:30-35. ISSN: 1844-7007

[8] Erdem M. Devlet Borçları. 7th ed. Bursa: Ekin Press; 2016. p. 169. ISBN: 975-7338-07-9

[9] Günay Bekar A. Devlet Borçlarının Sınıflandırılması. In: Tüğen K, Egeli H, Tandırcıoğlu H, editors. Devlet Borçları. İzmir: Kitabana Press; 2018. pp. 49-88. ISBN: 978-605-9515-27-6

[10] JMPC. Module 3: Public Expenditure and Public Debt [Internet]. 2018. Available from: www.jmpcollege.org/downloads/module3.pdf [Accessed: Oct 11, 2018]

[11] Saman RM. Productive and unproductive debt spending of microloans taken by urban borrowers (Johannesburg) [thesis]. South Africa: University of Pretoria; 2007

[12] Muley R. Public Debt: Meaning, Classification and Method of Redemption [Internet]. Available from: www.economicsdiscussion.net/debt-2/public-debt-meaning-classification-and-method-of-redemption/17472 [Accessed: Oct 10, 2018]

[13] İnce M. Devlet Borçlanması (Kamu Kredisi). 5th ed. Ankara: Seçkin Press; 1996. p. 376. ISBN: 975-347-090-8

[14] Işık AK, Karayılmazlar E. In: Organ İ, Işık H, editors. Devlet Borçları. Bursa: Ekin Press; 2005. p. 162. ISBN: 975-8768-677

[15] Demirhan H. Devlet Borçlarının Etkileri. In: Tüğen K, Egeli H, Tandırcıoğlu H, editors. Devlet Borçları. İzmir: Kitabana Press; 2018. ISBN: 978-605-9515-27-6

[16] Bülbül D. Devlet Borçlanmasının Sosyal ve Ekonomik Etkileri. Ekonomik Yaklaşım [Internet]. Available from: http://docplayer.biz.tr/735044-Devlet-borclanmasinin-sosyal-ve-ekonomik-etkileri.html [Accessed: Oct 11, 2018]

[17] Sharp AM. Review: A general theory of public debt. The American Journal of Economics and Sociology. 1959;**19**(1):99-111

[18] Bingöl Ö. Dış Borç Sorunu Küreselleşme Sürecinde Gelişmekte Olan Ülkeler ve Türkiye. İstanbul: Derin Press; 2014. p. 374. ISBN-10: 6054993232

[19] Kovancılar B, Bursalıoğlu Aybarç S. Küresel Finansal Kriz ve Tobin Vergisi. Vol. 2. International Social Sciences Congress in the Balkans. pp. 907-924. ISBN: 978-975-7988-43-4

[20] Schulmeister SA. General Financial Transaction Tax: A Short Cut of the

Pros, the Cons and a Proposal. WIFO Working Paper. No: 344 [Internet]. Available from: www.econstor.eu/bitstream/10419/128890/1/wp_344.pdf [Accessed: Oct 11, 2018]

[21] Reinhart CM. Rogoff KS. The Forgotten History of Domestic Debt. The Economic Journal, 121. [Internet]. 2011. pp. 319-350. Available from: https://onlinelibrary.wiley.com/doi/epdf/10.1111/j.1468-0297.2011.02426.x [Accessed: Oct 11, 2018]

[22] Korkmaz B. Bir iktidar/güç araci olarak diş yardim ve diş borçlarin kullanilmasi: Osmanlı devleti'nden günümüze Türkiye'nin diş borçlan(dırıl)ma serüveni [thesis]. Turkey: Manisa Celal Bayar University (Supervisor. Aybarç, S.); 2018

Chapter 3

New Approaches in Public Budgeting

Elif Ayse Sahin İpek

Abstract

This study intends to evaluate the contributions of new budgetary approaches classified as (i) environment-friendly budgetary approach, (ii) citizen-centred budgetary approach, (iii) citizen's budget approach, (iv) participatory budget approach and (v) gender-responsive budgeting approach, to contemporary budgetary system implementations. Although emphasis is placed on establishing a relationship between costs and intentional outcomes when explaining performance within the sphere of contemporary budgetary system implementations, new budgetary approaches facilitate interpretation of performance on the basis of costs versus intended impacts. From this standpoint, the common and most significant merit of new budgetary approaches is that they serve for assuring accountability on the economic and social externalities created with the public budget, for not only the citizens that actively participate in the financing of public activities but also those who benefit from the services thus delivered.

Keywords: state budgeting, modern budgeting systems, externalities, public financial management, efficacy

1. Introduction

The public budget is redolent of a technical, quantitative text that refers to expenditures and revenue-collection decisions made in a given time frame at central or local levels of government. Yet, budget is not only a technical, but also a political text [1]. After all, the budget reflects the public preferences and priorities of those members of society who will be served by and included in funding of activities [2]. Given the competitive demands existing despite constrained resources, the budgetary process, namely the allocation of resources, may basically be expressed as a political undertaking that is shaped by the needs and preferences of the electorate, as perceived by politicians [3]. Accordingly, budgets prepared following a similar administrative course unvaryingly in almost any country are hardly unbiased and typically represent the predominant political climate and affairs [4].

The process of public budgeting has undergone a rigorous transformation depending on the degree of evolution achieved by the individual, society, politics and economy. While a budget was merely an instrument used to indicate how much a state would earn as income by occidental communities until the seventeenth century following the acquisition of the right to budgeting with introduction of Magna Carta in 1215, it has become rather of an instrument showing how much a state would spend beside detailed forecasts of revenue to be collected, from seventeenth century onwards. The conventional budgetary system was adopted and followed throughout this period, in alignment with the then pre-eminent conception of a neutral, impartial state that is exclusively responsible for offering full range of goods and services to the public domain served [5].

Following the Economic Depression of 1929, the inauguration of the theory and concept of functional state and hence the resources' running shear against the ever-increasing expenditures have led the budget to transform into a more sophisticated tool for the state to fulfil its primary roles and functions in a cost-effective manner, from a traditional instrument of governance, accustomed by practice especially after 1950s. Starting from this period, the emerging contemporary budgetary systems included the performance budget system, the program budget system, the planning-programming-budgeting system, the zero-based budgeting system and performance-based budgetary system.

The semantics used to describe this period went analogous with the performance concept, as an assertive of the 'value for money'. However, the concept of performance is a constantly growing and expanding umbrella term. The advancements in the theory and understanding of democracy and subsequent alterations in conceptions of economy and development have brought the requirement for assuring accountability on the part of individuals who assume and fulfil active roles in the financing of public services, with regard to the externalities caused by services delivered to the whole society within the budget and their long-term effects, in addition to rationalising the political decision-making process with an endeavour to manage and subdue concerns for cost-effectiveness.

Consequently, even in the proposals delivered by the contemporary budgetary systems, the public budget and policies were presumed to affect all individuals that collectively form up the community at more or less the same level [6]. The new approaches in budgetary systems aim to establish and maintain oversight on the effects of the budget on not only those involved in financing of public services, but also, those who benefit from such services, in addition to rationalising the political decision-making process with an endeavour to properly address and handle the concerns for cost-effectiveness.

These approaches present a range of novel perspectives that enhance and extend the meaning and context of the performance concept within the auspices of the notion of improving public performance, cherished by the existing budgetary systems, rather than introducing propositions for a new budgetary system.

2. Change in budgetary systems and transformation in the conception of performance

Budgeting, in its traditional fashion accustomed by practice, exhibits both rolling (i.e. continually updated to add a new period, once the most recent period ends) and incremental (i.e. showing marginal change from a previous year) properties. Budgets are typically arranged in cash basis of accounting. Their contents consist of line items [7]. The traditional budgetary system makes an outlay of expenditures by inputs/resources. In such system, the budget functions as a mechanism of fiscal control over public activities. The paramount advantage that such system delivers is in that it provides simplicity and facilitates for the control of public expenditures against input items in delicate detail [8].

The contemporary budgetary systems lay less importance on cost controls, but instead, more focus on cost-effectiveness and cost-efficiency. This stance requires investigation of what a casual citizen obtains as benefit from the program, rather than probing into detail with the actual cost of a program. However, investigation of cost under a limitation of resources is rather associated with how to obtain the greatest benefit versus the cost undertaken [9].

While the traditional budgetary system is not suitable for establishing the cost-outcome relation from the viewpoint of results delivered by the public, the contemporary budgetary systems allow for evaluating the result-oriented nature and quality of budget applications, by integrating performance parameters into the budgeting process. On the other hand, within the array of modern budgetary system applications so far implemented, the task of establishing the relation between costs and targeted outcomes for describing performance has gained wide acceptance and more importance, rendering economic, efficiency and effectiveness the major components of performance. In public perception of performance, the hegemony of 3E (economic, efficiency and effectiveness) is a phenomenon that is mostly criticised.

While 'economic' concentrates on the cost of inputs as an aspect of performance that assists the selection of most optimal input components, 'efficiency' is derived from the relation between the product (output) of a production process and the resources (input) consumed to realise the output. Effectiveness demands a comparison to be made between the realised and predicted outcome. However, the level of attainment of the predicted outcome with effectiveness concept does not take account of the externalising effects of the outcomes delivered by public. It is therefore essential that the said effects as caused by public activities should, as well, be considered. The efficacy concept has been proposed to denote the effects inflicted by a program upon a society [10].

A similar relation has been conceptualised by [11] as 'net effects'. According to this concept, a service program may have entailed to additional costs in other programs and within the community, in a broader perspective. For instance, expenditures allocated to development of roads and motorways may have principally aimed at pruning the time of travel, and hence achieved this objective of theirs. However, such objective may have been accomplished at the expense of extra environmental pollution. Consequently, in order for the net effects of a particular program to be measured in perfect accuracy, the need is eminent for correctly identifying and assessing the effects caused by the practical implementation of that program on private sector and other public programs in progress [11].

As a matter of fact, in most cases, the potential occurs for realisation of a program at cost of compromises in assurance of productivity and effectiveness, sustainability and gender mainstreaming. For this reason, there is the need for expanding the meaning and conceptual coverage of performance so as to cover, in addition to thrift, productivity and effectiveness, such budget-driven externalities as gender mainstreaming, sustainability and participation, as accommodated by the concept of efficacy, in order to induce a comprehensive and homogeneous perception of the term. Therefore, performance, as an umbrella term, should better be denoted with cost-efficacy rather than cost-effectiveness.

3. Theoretical background

The system analysis approach is generally used for explaining the concept of performance in the public sector. The system analysis converts inputs that are associated with organisations and their tasks into deliverables and outcomes in its own terms. This tool, which describes transformation from inputs to outcomes, was initially employed during early 1980s, by theoreticians of business management as part of an effort to shed some light upon the production problems in the manufacturing industry and then, adopted as well by non-for-profit organisations from late

1980s and early 1990s, onwards. During the time advancing thereupon, this model was started to be used widely by both public and private sector organisations for the purpose of elaborating the outcomes of their respective programs [12].

Manninget al. ([12], p. 14) suggest that the input-output-outcome relation, within a system approach narrowed to cover the perspective of public sector exclusively, in order to help determination of performance across governmental entities.

The definitions of input-output and outcomes can be made as follows [12]:

Inputs: mean the resources put up in use by public entities to obtain the desired outputs. Accordingly, inputs are comprised of intangible, abstract assets such as effort, capital, financial assets and intellectual holdings. It is possible to categorise inputs under two distinctive categories as financial and non-financial assets, where, 'non-financial inputs' purport effort, capital, commodities and services dedicated to production of services expressed in measurable units like pieces, lots and quality, and 'financial inputs', or in other words, costs, refer to the costs of inputs covered by public or tax expenditures. The above figure contains two separate input boxes to highlight the difference in between.

Public sector process: means structures, procedures and management arrangements with a broad application within the public sector. These basic arrangements pose significance in that they direct activities of the government in progress. Activities are intended to indicate certain tasks assumed by the public sector. Activities play a key role in transformation of resources into public services. The architecture of the public sector may either prove to be an obstacle against, or subvene the uplifting of the performance of coordination activity across such institutional arrangements as for the type, budgeting and accounting methods of public services, as well as choices made in particular reference to which services are to be outsourced, and, the production of which services is to be undertaken by the public sector.

Outputs: mean output derived from the direct measurement of output volume and associated quality characteristics.

Outcomes: refer to the outcomes caused by outputs realised by public entities and their effects on the general public, where, 'intermediate outcomes' represent the outcomes of outputs or activities attained in progression towards the achievement of final outcomes, and, the 'final outcomes' are the effects and/or consequences of the outputs or activities of the government on the society.

While outcomes are not under the control of public entities, they may be categorised under two separate headings as intermediate and final outcomes, or, alternatively, as intended and unintended outcomes, where, in the latter classification, 'intended outcomes' are the effects that the public sector intends to create over the society, through its outputs. The intentions of the public sector are the objectives with its activities as disclosed plainly to the general public. Accordingly, the intentions of the government are clearly manifested, for instance, through laws, formal policy statements and regulations.

Failure to attain the intended outcomes, or, in an alternative way of expression, occurrence of unintended outcomes is considered a 'risk of outcome'. Generally, the outcomes are not dependent upon activities of the government, only. Adverse weather conditions, acts of war and periods of economic stagnation may also entail to unintended outcomes, by influencing the outcomes in a negative way. Accordingly, the risk of outcome signifies the potential of external factors to influence the outcomes in a negative or positive manner [13].

In the meanwhile, it is important to note here that the system approach discussed above until this point is not a new development for the public sector.

Bradford et al. [14] have made a material distinction between the outputs and outcomes in public sector disclosures of services. According to the authors, it is possible to conceptualise the inputs used in production of public goods and services in the form of a vector (I). This vector (I) then changes into the vector (D), representing the 'direct outputs', with the production function. However, the authors underline that vector (D) does not in general constitute a thing or things of primary interest to the citizen-consumer. Therefore, citizens pay more attention to the vector (C), representing the outcomes of vector (D). Accordingly, the executives in the public sector tend to focus on obtaining the vector (D) out of vector (I), while citizens centre all their interest around vector C [14].

This systems analysis approach, which has been conceptualised from inputs towards outcomes in the public sector, has further been extended by Burkhead and Hennigan [15]. The authors have picked the environmental cleaning service rendered by local administrations and, moving thereon, made an assessment of the system implemented by the relevant department by further splitting it up to five basic factors. Accordingly, the resulting system was composed of five base vectors that were respectively lettered (E) to represent environmental effects, (I) to represent the input, (A) to represent the activities, (O) to purport output and finally (C), to symbolise outcomes for the citizen-consumer.

Environmental vector (E) is used to describe environmental conditions. These environmental conditions are described as the needs of citizens and social structuring—i.e. household income, traditions, residence—and the general structuring of economic activities carried out among the society. The *input vector* symbolises labour force and capital equipment. The onus appears to rest with the head of department to set and maintain the best optimal balance between labour and capital, both of which pose significance for the input vector. On the other hand, the decision-making ability of the executive is shaped into a final form according to the budgetary limitations and legal regulations, as well as best practices, as in the case for private sector organisations.

The *activities vector* purports the stage during which important decisions are taken. As a matter of fact, the manner in which resources are to be consumed and hence the quantity and quality of public services are elaborated in the light of these decisions. The output vector, on the other hand, is an expression of clear and measurable outcomes of the activities performed in pursuance of the decisions made (namely, of the activities vector). The outcomes vector, however, does not consist of the numerical sum of the outputs vector. Accordingly, the outcomes of incremental growth in the environmental vector, for instance, may take the form of more municipal waste and garbage collected in response to dirtier streets. Therefore, albeit a productivity increase in public services, the efficiency of these services may have degraded drastically [15].

While this five-vector system analysis approach is capable of explaining the complex relations inherent in provision of public services, it fails to assess the efficiency of services provided. For this reason, Burkhead and Hennigan felt the need for another vector, the so-called 'social state vector'. The rationale behind this new vector lies in that citizens may have either improved or worsened conditions of living, as a result of a certain public service delivered.

In respect of the five vectors, productivity is the ratio of inputs to outputs, or inputs to activities, while efficiency in the public sector denotes the relationship between inputs and the social state vector. The social state vector requires consideration of two additional factors. The first of these is spatial dispersion, which is important for each local government service. In theory, the real revenue share and distribution within a municipal administration is influenced not only by taxes and those public activities expressed in the form of transfers, but also, by the manner in which the service is rendered. A district within the same municipal borders may receive better cleaning services compared to others. This may lead to an increase or decrease in real revenues of that particular municipal district. The second factor is neighbourhood participation. In the viewpoint of the authors, assuring participation of the public in decision-making processes is as vital as conduct/performance of services, in deployment and implementation of the social state [15]. At this point, concluding that long-term outcomes have been conceptualised as approximation to a social state by Burkhead and Hennigan [15] would not be a wrong approach.

4. New approaches in budgeting

The approaches to public budgeting, which facilitates due consideration of the budget at planning, preparation, approval, application and supervisory stages also with consideration of economic and social externalities caused by public activities, consist of (i) environmentally sensitive budgeting approach, (ii) citizen-centred budgetary approach, (iii) citizen's budget approach, (iv) participatory budget approach and (v) gender-responsive budgeting approach. The following section will describe the characteristic traits and integration into the basic budgeting processes of these approaches.

4.1 Environmentally sensitive budgeting approaches

In this part of the study, green budgeting and ecoBUDGET approaches are discussed under environmentally sensitive budgeting.

4.1.1 Green budgeting

The green budget, or efforts for integrating environmental concerns in fiscal processes of the public, is relatively new in the historical timeline. For decades, countries have been working for attaining their political goals on environment, utilising financial instruments. The mindset lying behind the green budget assumes that economic welfare of the future would depend on green technologies. These efforts bring along the ecological modernisation as a concept, thus envisaging approaches for economic growth bundled with environmental sustainability, based on a win-win strategy [16].

Green budgets are grounded on a careful consideration of environmental sensitivities in time of determination of the composition and magnitudes of expenditure and revenue items of the state budget and preparation of informed forecasts thereof. Budgets affect activities concerning the environment in various different ways, through their expenditure, revenue and neutral items, namely, those instructions that facilitate transition between funds. Public expenditures may yield positive externalities and positive impacts on the environment, when they support positive economic behaviour in general. Public revenues, on the other hand, are rather allocated to actions deterring activities that are generally detrimental to the environment. Such purposes are predominantly associated with application of environmental taxes [17].

The budgeting process typically starts with planning of areas of expenditure by prioritisation. The second stage oftentimes involves approval of the budget by the parliament, on submission by the finance ministers. The legislative body may superimpose additional environmental or non-environmental conditions to groupings of expenditure by type, subject to constitutional arrangements made at national level. The third stage is the implementation phase of the budget. In the course of budget implementation, expenditures are made by means of the central government, local or regional administrations, EU bodies and NGOs. The fourth stage comprises monitoring, final assessment and reporting, handled either by the spending department or by external auditing functions. This is the phase where environmental expenditures are assessed for efficiency and efficacy, together with all other expenditures. The first four stages usually result in an increase in revenues, which is then taken into account during the planning efforts for the next budget period [17].

4.1.2 ecoBUDGET

The ecoBUDGET is an environmental management tool designed specifically for and in joint action with local authorities, by the International Council for Local Environmental Initiatives (ICLEI), upon disclosure of its name for the first time in 1994, in the context of the Aalborg Charter, which may as well be used by all levels of government. The ecoBUDGET has been originally put forth as a project, mainly inspired by the idea that air, potable water, biodiversity and other similar natural resources can and must be managed with due care and diligence at the same level with financial resources [18].

The basic idea follows the assumption that natural resources can be managed in the same way financial resources, such as money, are managed, for the development of a sustainable society, by rendering smart allocation of resources easier. By doing so, it enables more productive management of resources on a local scale, based on a prioritisation of natural resources for use. Besides, it contributes to accountability in the political decision-making process, by way of budgeting and evaluation of natural resources [19]. In this sense, ecoBUDGET is a tool that enables the budgeting of environmental assets, in the same way followed for creating a financial budget for environmental assets. With this tool, the local governments may monitor their already scarce natural resources prospectively, and set objectives for these resources [20].

The ecoBUDGET approach relies on three fundamental principles: first of all, the environment-friendly budget circulation is highly dependent upon the fiscal budgeting principles and procedures that form up the guidance for individual methodological stages. Second of all, the plan encompasses the Deming Cycle (a.k.a. PDCA cycle), which was first introduced in 1956, as a continuous quality improvement model consisting of a logical sequence of four repetitive steps for continuous improvement and learning: plan, do, check and act, in its entirety. This cycle adopted by ecoBUDGET finds wide acceptance in environmental management systems. Third of all, the plan aims at sustainable growth. In this sense, the targets set and actions performed as part of ecoBUDGET must contribute to sustainability. It is for this reason why, a strong political commitment and community involvement are pre-requisites for ecoBUDGET [21].

The ecoBUDGET cycle reflects the three fundamental stages of the financial budgeting cycle: budgetary planning, budget application and balancing of the budget. At the end of the year, full disclosure is made about the environmental status [22]. The budget balance and the performance analysis to be provided in its attachment will support the next year's budget with vital information and data, and be rendered more effective and better prepared in a loop. The most prominent feature ecoBUDGET is that it is tightly attached to continuous improvement and supports learning organisations in a cyclic approach [21].

According to ICLEI [21], preparation and approval of the budget consists of: (i) a unit or function should be formed and appointed to assume full responsibility for coordinating and implementing the ecoBUDGET process. Such unit or function preferably be an autonomous, interdisciplinary ecoBUDGET Coordination Team (or environment budget department); (ii) a framework should be developed for executive instructions and internal audits, in addition to the reporting frame and guidelines; (iii) a preliminary report should be drawn that properly addresses the changes expected in both environmental consumption and in legal and political structure; (iv) the ecoBUDGET is prepared, consisting of three essential documents including the main environment budget, declaration of environmental assets and an environment-benefit analysis; and (v) approval of the main environment budget finalises the preparatory stage.

Implementation of the budget consists of (i) measurement management referring to the responsibilities and programs for individual indicators that must be agreed upon within the administration, (ii) accounting in full support of mechanisms for monitoring and reporting of individual indicators enables early detection of whether environmental budget figures are complied, and (iii) feedback given to the senior management on all major expenditures to enable timely realisation of necessary corrections or gain political legitimacy through parliamentary bills.

Evaluation stage consists of (i) the budget balance for the period which is reached with compilation of annual accounts from individual accounts, (ii) the internal audit that verifies and validates how close the administration is to attaining the predefined objectives, by comparing annual balance with long-term objectives, (iii) the approval of budgetary outcomes which follows a similar stance to the approval of the main budget.

The ecoBUDGET follows a cyclic pattern that is identical with financial budgeting. In ecoBUDGET approach, however, indicators and accounts are not assigned with monetary values. In the event that natural resources are expressed in monetary terms, practice will delimit the opinions of politicians with financial indicators, instead of assuming comprehensive responsibility with respect to natural resources. Additionally, this will be accompanied by the problem of unintentional off-setting of miscellaneous environmental impacts from one another. Yet, based on the probability that measures taken with respect to conservation of natural resources may cause either a rise or drop in initial investment costs and operating overheads, a relation exists between ecoBUDGET and the fiscal budget. Therefore, mutual relations between budgets should be considered at inception stage and further be included in reviews during the decision-making process [21].

4.2 Citizen-centred budget

Citizen-centred budgeting is a budgeting approach, which seeks to ensure participation of the citizens in the budgeting process, across approval, implementation, auditing and evaluation phases of budgeting whether directly in person or by officially assigned proxies [8].

Although it was originally brought forward to strengthen accountability, citizen-centred budgeting is not meant for this singular purpose. The inefficiency particularly in distribution of resources, in combination with lack of ability to allocate resources based on needs, and the poor functioning of the government due to this fact are indicated among the other matters addressed by the citizen-centred budgeting approach [23].

Accordingly, the approach aims to insure a more efficient redistribution of resources, by including citizens in the process of budgeting, through the citizen's budget initiatives. These initiatives are expected to slacken the budgeting process a bit further and render the decisions made more acceptable, by enabling and encouraging full participation of citizens in the process. The citizen-centred budgeting also brings the opportunity for citizens to assess the overall performance of their government, voice their complaints, and take action towards tackling the odds.

It is necessary to make effective institutional changes to make budget and budgetary processes citizen-oriented. This can be accomplished by two ways; a representative institutional structure or a mechanism enabling participation should be established [23].

The steps to be followed in creating the citizen-centred budget can be enumerated as follows [24]:

i. take due account of comments raised by the advisory board that is formed up by citizens regarding services,

ii. take due account of the results of citizen's satisfaction surveys, in time of budget preparation,

iii. afterwards, let the administration present their proposals for the budget,

iv. have the executive in the agency revise and reshape the goals and objectives with the services in accordance with the advisory board's comments, citizen's wishes in citizen's satisfaction surveys and further advice and suggestions of the administration.

v. make sure that the said goals and objectives are properly included in the budget in time of preparation, establishing a goal-objective association with the resources,

vi. once this stage is completed, have the executives meet with the council or committees of the city that represent citizens in a preplanned and timely disclosed gathering for reviewing the budget rates,

vii. following such review, make sure that mechanisms of accountability are properly defined, before the budget takes its final form and is approved,

viii. forthwith upon implementation of the budget, make sure that reports are drawn on intended outcomes as predetermined, for exchange of information with the general public.

4.3 Citizen's budget

Citizen's budget is an extension of citizen-centred budgeting [23]. Its first introduction to public life dates back to 1932, when it was initiated as a non-governmental organisation acting under the title Citizen's Budget Commission in the United States, with primary engagement consisted of inspections conducted for the potential production of new sources of income by cutting the costs of city governance, on commission and assignment of the merchants, bankers and real estate industry representatives of the day. The adverse effects of the Economic Depression of 1929 hitting the New York City's Municipal Administration further elevated the importance of the Citizen's Budget Commission. Since 2008, there have been notable developments with national governments in the trend towards improvement and publication of citizen's budget [25].

The citizen's budget has been designed to present basic financial information to a general group of random citizens. The citizen's budget is a simpler, non-technical illustration of the public budget. It was developed for building a general sense and knowledge among citizens on what public plans are meant to be and how financial resources are distributed. This version briefs the reader/beneficiary on public financial resources, revenues, expenses and other information as may be considered relevant or vital. This straightforward guide meant for assisting the citizens shows where the public resources were spent and how, and to what extent the needs and expectations of the government were satisfied in return, within a given time period [23].

The citizen's budget can be produced by non-governmental organisations or other defence groups; however, it should be developed and published by governments, since it institutionalises the commitment of governments to clearly present their policies to the general public [26].

The citizen's budget should be prepared within a prearranged plan and through consultations with its potential users. Because it is one of the paramount goals of the citizen's budget, which requires a system that works for annual periods in an orderly manner, to encourage citizens for participating in debates and discussions on the budget, it should be presented and disclosed in a time frame that allows for such participation. In other words, a citizen's budget version of the budget in draft should have been published on the same day in which the draft itself is published. Likewise, the citizen's budget version of the appropriation act should be produced as soon as possible after approval of the budget by legislature. All the above versions of the citizen's budget should be published and disseminated by exploiting all available communication channels, once after being produced [27].

The general context of the citizen's budget to be prepared in line with the foregoing principles should be designed in five parts. The first part should include an introduction and provide an overview of the basic concepts, while the second part should include the economic conjuncture and the government's goals, with the third part making a categorisation of expenditures by institutional, functional and economic nature, along with an evaluation of sources of income within the sphere of taxes and indebtedness. The last two parts may contain projections of fiscal administration and general economic structure, with an analysis of opportunities, threats and action to be taken there against [25].

4.4 Participatory budgeting

There is not a clear definition adopted in consensus for the concept and understanding of participatory budgeting. Studies performed on participatory budgeting approach follow practical implementations [28]. The scale at which the participatory budgeting approach is applicable may vary from central to local governments and municipal administrations [29].

The participatory budgeting approach was initially put in action by the Municipal Administration of the City of Porto Alegre in Brazil, 1989, and thence spread across several parts of the world, from 2000s, after inspiring similar projects in numerous cities of Brazil. Participatory budgeting is a public budgeting approach that allows for direct participation of community members in a democratic process, for first-hand experience [5].

The participatory budgeting approach is notable for the fact that it builds upon two distinct needs: improving public performance and enhancing the quality of democracy. At this context, the participatory budgeting approach helps betterment of public performance through a series of rules that restrict and tend to control the privileges of the public administration, while boosting opportunities for citizens to participate in debates and discussions on public policies. It helps with further enhancement of the quality of democracy by encouraging direct participation of citizens in public political discussions, to help them move beyond consultative deliberation and into the realm of state-sanctioned decision-makers [30].

The rudimentary course of progress that must essentially be followed in participatory budgeting consists of (i) identification, (ii) discussion, (iii) decision-taking, (iv) execution and (v) monitoring. Identification involves (i) identification of needs that the agency may reveal during the participatory budgeting process, (ii) identification of citizens to receive services that fit in the needs so identified, (iii) identification of the manner in which such services are to be performed and projects drawn in relation thereto, (iv) establishment of the committees to be responsible for these services, and (v) setting and scheduling of the times for meetings of the committees so established. Discussion consists of two stages, namely: (i) election by committees of service projects and (ii) identification of feasible projects with top priority. Decision-making involves (i) a vote on projects to be selected and (ii) approval of the projects thus selected. Following this stage, the projects selected during the execution phase will be executed by the relevant public authority in charge. During the supervision phase, execution of selected projects will be checked and supervised by citizens [5].

The core principles of participatory budgeting can be listed, as follows [30]:

i. Administration should be split in such a manner that provides ease for distribution of resources and the conduct of meetings by regions, service topics or amount of resources to be allocated, depending on the scale at which participatory budgeting is executed.

ii. Throughout the year, government-led meetings shall be held to address different aspects of budgeting and policy creation cycles. Dissemination of information through these meetings will be followed by policy proposals, discussions on proposals, selection of policies as proposed as well as of the delegations to attend them, ending with the inspection/review phase.

iii. Each administration concocts its own formulation to guarantee fair distribution of resources (social justice), depending on the scale at which the participatory budgeting approach will be executed.

iv. Discussions will be staged between the participants themselves and participants and related functions of government on resources and policies. Proxies will be assigned from among the participants.

v. These proxies will pay visits to all project groups confirmed first beforehand the final vote. Such visits will allow for assessing the degree by which the proposed projects are capable of coping with the social requirements, by the delegates.

vi. All elected representatives will have a right to vote in all selected projects.

vii. A council will be set up and operational with participation of two representatives from each region that falls within the reference and authority frames of the municipal administration. This council will then hold regular meetings with the management of the relevant functional branch, in order to perform an oversight of the participatory budgeting program.

viii. Once approved by proxies of the participatory budget, the budget will be submitted by the mayor to the ultimate statutory decision-making body, and such body will issue its final approval to give full effect to the participatory budget.

ix. The year-end report will provide information on the outcomes of the public works and programs executed.

x. Regional/sectoral committees will be set up for the purpose of monitoring the execution of policy proposals.

At this extent, the participatory budgeting approach stiffens the resolve for a more proactive civil society by enabling the active participation of citizens in public budget and thereby self-education and improvement in the area of budgeting. Participatory budgeting also helps encouraging transparency, which has a vast potential to alleviate the risks of inefficiency and fraud in public governance. It delivers the opportunity for those citizens who were historically excluded from taking part in what participatory budgeting approach has to offer in the past, mostly due to low levels of income generated and education received, to make choices that would influence their government's course of conduct against them. In this sense, the participatory budgeting approach facilitates access for historically excluded citizens to major decision-taking mechanisms [30].

The participatory budgeting programs exist in two basic forms. One is the 'participatory budget for public affairs', and the other is the 'thematic participatory budgeting' method, where the former, 'participatory budget for public affairs' concentrates on certain public projects and ensures participation of citizens in decision-making processes related with investments allocated exclusively for these projects. The thematic participatory budgeting, on the other hand, focuses rather on general policies on government expenditures. Such policies lay focus on more general trends such as allocation of increasing public expenditures to a certain health-care scheme. The meetings of concern are inclined to lure more informed activists with higher potential to become part of a theme-based social movement [30].

4.5 Gender-responsive budgeting

Gender-responsive budgeting, also referred to as 'gender budgeting', 'women's budget' or 'gender-based budgeting' through citations in scholarly articles [31], or as GRB in short, deals with how differentiating needs of men and women that collectively form up the society should be fulfilled, by incorporating a gender perspective at all levels of budgetary process and restructuring revenues and expenditures in order to promote gender equality [32].

Acknowledgement of the fact that macroeconomic policies play an important role for their outcomes affecting the living standards and economic opportunities of an entire population in general, and women in particular, helps justify the rationale behind incorporation of a gender perspective at all levels of budgetary process. In this sense, the fact that macroeconomic policies coerce lower levels of production and obliterate growth of personal skills instead of diminishing, if not eliminating, social inequality, gives rise to extra cost burdens in terms of lessened spare times and damage caused to levels of welfare [33]. The basic thought that underlies the efforts for GRB emanates from the urgent need for public policies and budgets to make a more distinctive notion of the mainstreaming effect. This will help decision-makers in becoming more qualified and more comprehensively informed, and thus developing healthier policies on the matter [4].

First implications of GRB analyses were noted in a structure backed by an analysis of the impacts of initially federal and then state-wide expenditures of the government on women, performed in Australia, during 1980s. This practice was furthered by South Africa and the Philippines in mid 1990s. The UN Conference held in Beijing, 1995 has led to the spreading of public interest in gender-responsive budgeting analyses and gender-responsive budgeting among numerous governments and women's organisations and increased number of initiatives covering the matter [34]. At this point, the conference in Beijing propounded opinions in favour of incorporating the gender perspective in budgetary decisions affecting public policies and schemes. Another opinion voiced in the same platform has been about rendering governments accountable for their commitments to gender equality. Thus, gender-responsive budgeting is viewed as a crucial mechanism for the planning, budgeting and execution of governments' commitments on gender equality and monitoring of the progress and outcomes of such commitments in action [35].

When the time arrived at year 2000 on the calendar, the UN announced the Millennium Development Goals, defining a total of eight goals, including two, exclusively addressing women. These goals as aforementioned have been identified as promotion of gender equality and empowerment of women and improvement of maternal health. In one of the activities performed in line with these goals, the UN Commission on the Status of Women has held its 52nd session in 2008, on the subject of 'Financing for Gender Equality and Empowerment of Women' [36]. This session resulted in the joint resolve for ensuring 'conduct of all gender mainstreaming analyses of all revenues and expenditures and preparation of gender-based budgets for promoting gender equality in the society' [37].

Currently, a diversified range of variants of gender-based budgeting are being attempted to be executed in over 80 countries, in which attempts vary greatly from country to country. Some countries have adopted fiscal policies and programs aimed at closing the gap in social gender mainstreaming and promotion of the progression of women, as part of their social gender budgeting efforts. Others have started to consolidate information in a systematic manner, on women's diversified needs and the differentiating effects of fiscal policies on women and men. Only a few countries have so far succeeded in realising radical changes in both fiscal policies and complementary administrative campaigns. As a matter of fact, the most affluent efforts comprise both political and administrative aspects. However, a vast majority of these efforts appear to be entangled by the lack of commitments by fiscal policy-makers and by bureaucracy and the weaknesses resident in structuring and implementation of initiatives. Moreover, some other countries have consistently failed in getting beyond setting up administrative authorities to deal with the touching matters, or, alternatively, organising instructional courses for public servants [38].

Basically, the GRB is composed of two stages. The first is the analysis of budget from a gender perspective. The second is reconsideration of budgetary decisions with a gender perspective. While initial stage requires both comprehensive data and a strong analytic capacity to analyse such data, the second stage urges incorporation of gender perspective in the budgetary process.

When conducting an analysis of budgetary effects on women and men, the budget expenses can be divided into three categories as (i) gender-based expenditures, (ii) expenditures for equal opportunities and (iii) core expenditures. The *gender-based expenditures* are concerned with the specific needs of women (or men). For instance, programs on women's health, counselling on domestic violence, special campaigns addressing women mothering toddlers or special education campaigns for girls can be assessed to fall in this category. Expenditures of this type need not aim gender equality. *Equal opportunity expenditures* are those aimed at promoting gender equality, such as paid maternity leaves and child care support allowances. Core expenditures are considered gender independent and form 99% of the total government expenditures. Therefore, analysing the differential effects of expenditures of this type on women and men poses particular importance [39].

In application, the gender-based analysis classifies the public revenues under five major categories. These include tax revenues (direct and indirect taxes), benefit taxes such as fees and charges, intergovernmental aids and borrowings [40]. Those items that need to be analysed with respect to tax revenues under the title of gender can be sorted as the revenue distribution effects of the taxation system, magnitude of the tax base, tax composition, tax management and sexual discrimination in application of tax rates [39]. Revenues such as charges, duties and prices which are received in return for a benefit can be determined based on gender, on most occasions. Consequently, it will be easy to measure their effects on gender equality. Assessing the public revenues received through intergovernmental grants will be as easy as the latter, if provision of the grant is brought conditional upon discouragement and elimination of sexual discrimination [40]. Revenues generated through borrowing arrangements are hard to assess for their effects on women and men. This demands for an analysis of future debt burden caused by women and men, separately [39].

Every step of the budgetary process bears a significant potential for integration of budget preparation, approval, execution, auditing and assessment with GRB and the decision-making process. The budget preparation, which is the first stage of the budgetary process, is generally the task of the executive authority. The gender mainstreaming perspective can be incorporated into the budget planning phase by means of (i) gender-specific budget initiatives specified under the government's budget policy, (ii) incorporation of gender mainstreaming policies in general guidelines for budget preparation and (iii) identification of gender-specific priorities for each spending branch/unit in time of budgetary allocations held at ministerial level. Once after the budget preparatory phase is completed, the draft budget will be submitted to legislature, for approval. For incorporating the gender equality perspective into this stage, a number of suggestions have been raised, such as (i) organisation of gender-responsive guides identifying the general framework in expenditure and revenue arrangements for legislative decisions, (ii) popularisation of gender-responsive language in law texts rendered by legislature for creating and introducing new programs and agencies, (iii) making use of GRB guides in arbitrary allocation of resources, and (iv) superimposition of the requirement for inserting efficacy assessments of gender mainstreaming efforts, into financial statements, through introduction of new laws on expenditure and revenues [41].

During the budget implementation phase, it may be useful to (i) create guidelines for expenditures left exclusively to the discretion of ministries by legislature, (ii) develop rules based on gender mainstreaming for outsourcing, supply and payment allocation processes, and (iii) application of gender goals in selection and recruitment of employees, for incorporating the gender equality perspective. The budgetary controls shall be performed by the court of accounts on behalf of legislature. Such controls will be deemed to cover financial, compliance and performance checks. (i) Incorporation of gender aspect in financial checks with emphasis placed on expenditures and compliance, (ii) inclusion of gender aspect in performance checks with focus on outputs and outcomes, and (iii) the checking for and supervision of compliance with gender goals and rules are among recommendations spelt out for integration of the gender perspective into the budgetary process [41].

5. Conclusion(s)

In this study, (i) environment-friendly budgetary approach, (ii) citizen-centred budgetary approach, (iii) citizen's budget approach, (iv) participatory budget approach and (v) gender-responsive budgeting approach were assessed for the perspectives they bring upon the budgetary process.

The environment-friendly budgeting approaches consist of approaches proposing the establishment of a link in between the public expenditures and revenues on one hand and environmental resources on the other, in reaching the goal of sustainable economic growth and development. Of these approaches, the green budget approach suggests that the effects of budget on revenue and expenditure components be considered, while the ecoBUDGET alternative proposes separate budgeting of the natural resources aside from the fiscal budget and without using monetary values.

The citizen-oriented or citizen-based budgeting allows for inclusion of citizens' service performance assessments in the budgetary process, while the citizen's budget makes it possible for citizens to gain a fair level of budget literacy. Participatory budgeting enables direct participation of citizens in budgetary decision-making process.

Gender-responsive budgeting envisages the incorporation of gender equality perspective into the budgetary process, and supports preparation, approval, execution and supervision of budgets in a mindset that investigates the effects of the budget on women and men, as well as on boys and girls.

With the above-mentioned perspectives, they bring forward what the new budgeting approaches share in common, among others and is that they all add a new dimension to the perception of 'performance', as revealed by the contemporary budgeting systems, in the budgetary process, instead of delivering propositions for novel budgetary systems.

In this context, the implementations of contemporary budgeting systems seem to employ frequent repetitions of the 'value for money' when describing performance and support successful attempts on raising awareness among those who are actively involved in financing of public activities, on cost-efficiency. The new budget approaches help expanding the concept and context of performance from the point it covers cost-efficiency towards cost-efficacy, to be thenceforth defined as the level of progress achieved by public activities in 'intended effects' instead of 'actual outcomes' obtained. Doing so would make it possible to base budgetary decision-making process upon social and economic externalities of public expenditure and revenue items. This is meaningful especially for unveiling the idea that public performance is not just a matter of tax payers only, but in fact a concern of all other citizens who may not have registered their names as tax-payers for this or that reason, as well. Apart from this, new approaches inferred also possess significance for supporting the notion of developing accountability of the contemporary budgetary systems, because of their profound ability to allow for a better understanding among those who partake in the financing of public activities, of the positive externalities brought forward by financial contributions.

Author details

Elif Ayse Sahin İpek
Department of Public Finance, Faculty of Economics and Administrative, Sciences
İzmir Katip Çelebi University, İzmir, Turkey

*Address all correspondence to: elifa.sahin.ipek@ikc.edu.tr

References

[1] Akduran Ö. 5018 sayılı Kanun ve Kamu İdarelerinde Cinsiyete Duyarlı Bütçeleme. In: Altug F, Kesik A, Seker M, editors. Kamu Bütçesinde Yeni Yaklaşımlar. 1st ed. Ankara: Seckin; 2013. pp. 19-36

[2] Altug F. Kamu Bütçesi. Bursa: Filiz; 2004

[3] McCay A. Developing a gender budge initiative: A question of process or policy? Lessons learned from the Scottish experience. University of Linz Gender Studies Series. 2004. [Internet] Available from: http://www.infopolis.es/web/GenderBudgets/pdf/GB_Scotland.pdf [Accessed: 24-10-2018]

[4] Sugiyama N, Hall B. Gendered Budget Work in the Americas: Selected Country Experiences. Austin: University of Texas; 2002

[5] Meric M. Bütçe Sistemlerinde Dönüşüm ve Değişim. In: Altug F, Kesik A, Seker M, editors. Kamu Bütçesinde Yeni Yaklaşımlar. 1st ed. Ankara: Seckin; 2013. pp. 155-171

[6] Budlender D, Sharp R, Allen K. How to do a Gender-Sensitive Budget Analysis: Contemporary Research and Practice. London: Australian Agency for International Development, Canberra and the Commonwealth Secretariat; 1998

[7] Wilsdavsky A. A budget for all seasons? Why the traditional budget lasts. Public Administration Review. 1978;**39**(6):501-509

[8] Shah A, Shen C. Citizen-centric performance budgeting at the local level. In: Shah A, editor. Local Budgeting. The World Bank Public Sector Governance and Accountability Series. Washington: The World Bank; 2007. pp. 151-178

[9] Rubin I. Budget formats: Choices and implications. In: Shah A, editor. Local Budgeting. The World Bank Public Sector Governance and Accountability Series. Washington: The World Bank; 2007. pp. 131-150

[10] Flynn A, Grey A, Jenkins W, Rutherford B. Making indicators perform. Public Money and Management. 1986;**8**(4):35-41

[11] Beeton D. Justifying departmental expenditure programmes. Public Money. 1986;**6**(3):43-47

[12] Manning N, Kraan J, Malinska J. How and Why Government Activity Be Measured in "Government at a Glance". OECD GOV Technical Paper 1, OECD Project on Management in Government: Comparative Country Data, GOV/PGC(2006)10/ANN1. 2006

[13] OECD. Result Focused Management and Budgeting: Working Definitions [Internet]. Available from: http://www.oecd.org/dataoecd/59/28/1851320.pdf [Accessed: 24-10-2018]

[14] Bradford DF, Malt RA, Oates WE. The rising cost of local public services: Some evidence and reflections. National Tax Journal. 1969;**22**(2):185-202

[15] Burkhead J, Hennigan PJ. Productivity analysis: A search for definition and order. Public Administration Review. 1978;**38**(1):34-40

[16] Russel D, Benson D. Green budgeting in an age of austerity: A translatlantic comparative perspective. Environmental Politics. 2014;**23**(2):243-262

[17] Tandircioglu H, Yapici F. Küreselleşme Sürecinde Postmodern Bütçe Yaklaşımlarına Toplu Bir Bakış. Vergi Raporu. 2016;**206**:38-62

[18] ICLEI. ecoBUDGET Guide for Asian Local Authorities. Dynamic Enterprises,

2007 [Internet] Available from: http://webcentre.ecobudget.org/fileadmin/user_uploads/ecobudget-Asia_final.pdf [Accessed: 24-10-2018]

[19] ecoBUDGET. About ecoBUDGET [Internet]. Available from: http://webcenter.ecobudget.org/about-ecobudget [Accessed: 24-10-2018]

[20] ecoBUDGET. [Internet]. Available from: http://webcenter.ecobudget.org/home [Accessed: 24-10-2018]

[21] ICLEI. The ecoBUDGET Guide. Sweden: Waxjö; 2004

[22] ecoBUDGET. ecoBUDGET Cycle [Internet]. Available from: http://webcenter.ecobudget.org/why-ecobudget/ecobudget-cycle [Accessed: 24-10-2018]

[23] Uysal Ö, Sahin M. Vatandaş Odaklı Bütçeleme ve Vatandaş Bütçe. In: Altug F, Kesik A, Seker M, editors. Kamu Bütçesinde Yeni Yaklaşımlar. 1st ed. Ankara: Seckin; 2013. pp. 237-254

[24] Stampfler M. Citizen-based budgeting. Public Management. 2005;**87**(10):20-24

[25] Seker M, Beynam H. Vatandaş Bütçesi ve Uygulama Örnekleri. In: Altug F, Kesik A, Seker M, editors. Kamu Bütçesinde Yeni Yaklaşımlar. 1st ed. Ankara: Seckin; 2013. pp. 221-235

[26] International Budget Partnership. Citizens Budget [Internet]. Available from: http://www.internationalbudget.org/open-budget-survey/resources-for-government/citizens-budgets/ [Accessed: 24-10-2018]

[27] International Budget Partnership. The Power of Making it Simple: A Government Guide to Developing Citizens Budget. 2012. [Internet] Available from: www.internationalbudget.org [Accessed: 24-10-2018]

[28] Moynihan DP. Citizen participation in budgeting: Prospects for developing countries. In: Shah A, editor. Participatory Budgeting. The World Bank Public Sector Governance and Accountability Series. Washington: The World Bank; 2007. pp. 55-87

[29] Gilman HR. Engaging Citizens: Participatory Budgeting and the Inclusive Governance Movement within the United States. Cambridge: Harvard Kennedy School Ash Center for Democratic Governance and Innovation; 2016

[30] Wampler B. A guide to participatory budgeting. In: Shah A, editor. Participatory Budgeting. The World Bank Public Sector Governance and Accountability Series. Washington: The World Bank; 2007. pp. 21-54

[31] Bartle JR. The potential of gender budgeting: Has its day come? In: Panel on Democratizing the Budgetary Process. Association for Budgeting and Financial Management Annual Conference; 12 October 2009; Kansas City, Missouri, USA

[32] Budlender D, Hewitt G. Engendering Budgets: A Practitioners' Guide to Understanding and Implementing Gender-Responsive Budgets. UK: Commonwealth Secretariat; 2003

[33] Villagomez E. Gender responsive budgets: Issues, good practices and policy options [Internet]. In: Regional Symposium on Mainstreaming Gender into Economic Policies; 28-30 January 2004. Available from: http://www.gsdrc.org/document-library/gender-responsive-budgets-issues-good-practices-and-policy-options/ [Accessed: 24-10-2018]

[34] Balmori HH. Gender and Budgets Overview Report. UK: Bridge; 2003

[35] Tugen K, Ozen A. Cinsiyete Duyarlı Bütçeleme Anlayışı. Maliye Dergisi. 2008;**154**:1-11

[36] Gunluk-Senesen G. Toplumsal Cinsiyete Duyarlı Bütçeleme: Türkiye İçin Bir Değerlendirme. In: Bütçe Sürecinde Parlamentonun Değişen Rolü Sempozyumu (8-9 Ekim 2008) Kitabı; Afyonkarahisar. 2008. pp. 1-13

[37] Gunluk-Senesen G. Toplumsal Cinsiyete Duyarlı Bütçeleme: Kapsam, Örnekler ve Türkiye İçin Öneriler. In: Altug F, Kesik A, Seker M, editors. Kamu Bütçesinde Yeni Yaklaşımlar. 1st ed. Ankara, Seckin; 2013. pp. 97-128

[38] Stotsky J. Gender Budgeting: Fiscal Context and Current Status. IMF Working Paper: WP/16/149. 2016

[39] Cansiz H. Cinsiyete Duyarlı Bütçeleme ve Türkiye'ye İlişkin Öneriler. Ankara: Gazi Kitabevi; 2009

[40] Isik A, Isik H. Sosyal Eşitsizliklerin Giderilmesinde Bir Çözüm Önerisi: Cinsiyet Esaslı Bütçeleme (Teori, Gelişim ve Uygulama). Sosyal Siyaset Konferansları Dergisi. 2010;**57**:167-211

[41] Rubin MM, Bartle JR. Integrating gender into government budgets: A new perspective. Public Administration Review. 2005:259-272

Section 2

Regional Examples of Public Economics and Finance

Chapter 4

Decentralized Territorial Communities and Implementation of Public Policies: The Case of Cameroon

Guy Yakana Yombi, Mounton Chouaïbou
and Lucie Yakana Agoume

Abstract

Cameroon's Constitutional Law of 18 January 1996 enshrined decentralization as a fundamental principle of the organization of state governance, and subsequent implementing legislation affirms the central government's commitment to transferring a number of powers to local authorities with a view to local management. Local and regional authorities then appear as an essential link in the implementation of public policies at the local level. Their genuine autonomy in financial and administrative matters is a necessary condition for achieving local development objectives. However, a review of the existing literature reveals that these communities do not have real autonomy in public policy decision-making, which is illustrated by mixed development at the local level.

Keywords: public policy, decentralization, territorial communities, local development, resources

1. Introduction

The binomial "local-national" is not only old, but it is also probably inherent in any state regardless of what it is. This duality can be translated by imbalances and tensions, but it commits necessary relations between the central authority and the local authorities, which is qualified of territorial community.

The expression territorial community refers to the decentralization that is called the territorial; the expression "public policy," with respect to it, returns to the state. With regard to African countries, the debate around the decentralization, although old, has taken the magnitude toward the end of 90 years. The foundation of the accentuation of this debate has been the approximation of the government of the local actors for involvement of the latter in the decisions of public policy for a better efficiency of the actions undertaken.

The achievement of the decentralization remains subject to the legal plan to the respect of three essential conditions: the existence of a sphere of specific skills for the benefit of the local communities; the taking in charge of local affairs by authorities at the base, independent of the central power both by their mode of designation; and the evaluation of their actions as for their revocation. The emphasis is on a sufficient autonomy of these local authorities in the management of their own affairs. Consequently, the decentralization assumes the existence and the accountability of the dismemberment of the state, spends the management of local affairs by officials and local elected representatives, and recognizes the relevance and the effectiveness of the management of proximity.

In the specific case of Cameroon, the decentralization has been endorsed by the Constitution of 1996 which made this country a unitary decentralized state. This implies the recognition of the existence of local communities and the maintenance of the unity of the state. Eight years later, a series of legal text have brought clarification on the objectives assigned to decentralization and the territorial communities whose emphasis is on the promotion of development at the local level. Furthermore, the laws of the decentralization of 2004 have redefined the relationship between the central government and the local authority in matters of public policy.

Entering an operational phase in 2010, the territorial communities are seen to transfer certain skills and the appropriate means to give impetus to the development at the local level through appropriate public policies. This article allows you to present the role played by the territorial communities in the implementation of public policies in the Cameroonian context. To achieve this, a documentary review is undertaken to identify the key concepts, present the characteristics of the decentralization of Cameroon, and state the role played by the territorial communities in the implementation of public policies.

2. Public policy: response of the political actors to a problem of society

In a given society, any problem can become a policy since the question is to know by what mechanisms. It is safe, in any case, that the triggering of the public action is not linked to any threshold of the intensity of the problem. For example, the relationship between the onset of policies for the protection of the environment in the year 1970 and the pollution of the era of the industrial revolution cannot be established. Even if we suppose the question of the identification of the problem resolved (everyone agrees today to consider that there are problems of pollution, delinquency, or poverty), it remains to be determined from what threshold of intensity public action should be triggered.

2.1 What is a public policy?

Public policies, the fact of the multiplicity of research work, are variously defined. However, these definitions are functions of the following elements: the actors and the activities as well as the problems and the solutions.

2.1.1 Anchor on the actors and their activities

The specialists of this current perception of public policies see the public policy as activities or absences of activities on the part of actors defined more or less precisely.

The public policy is defined as everything that the public authorities decide to do or not to do [1]. In other words, public policies are the actions undertaken by the government [2]. Other authors present government policies such as this that the political and administrative authorities, legitimately constituted, decide to do or not to do and what they are doing in reality [3]. Of this fact, they consist of a series of action or inaction, more than inactions or specific decisions.

These definitions emphasize the government actors (public authorities, political or administrative). They neglect the impact of other actors, members of political parties, electoral or administered populations, in the decision or the nondecision to make the public policies. It is to correct this failure that a definition involving all actors has appeared. As well, public policies are presented as the set of interrelated decision, taken by an actor or a group of political actor [4].

Other definitions are a complement with the emphasis on the subject of public policies.

2.1.2 Anchor on the problems and the solutions

When the object of public policy is defined in a precise way, the authors generally make a reference to the notions of problems or even to conflicts. These concepts allow you to make a clarification on the "stimuli," which seek to respond to the public policies. As well, public policies are actions or inactions in response to requirements [5]. It is also of actions oriented toward the settlement of a problem [6]. Another approach presents the public policies as a series of action or inaction that public authorities choose to adopt to solve a problem or an interlocking set of problems [7]. It is important to note that the stimuli to the origin of the public policies are internal or external to the system policy being, whereas the political system can be the object of an economic policy.

The purposes or the solutions sought are at the center of some of the definitions of public policies. In questioning the why of public policies, it appears that these are of the order of the project and includes values and practices sought [8]. The concept of purpose is also essential in the sense that public policies refer to the selection of goals and the means to achieve, therefore, in search of solutions [4].

A public policy may be presented as a set of activities (or non-activities) of public authorities (central, regional, or local) to provide solutions to the problems of society. This response consists of actions/public interventions through legislation, regulation, taxation, transfers, and public expenditure to meet a request from the community in a specific area.

2.2 Typology of public policies

History allows you to raise the fields, actions, means, and objectives of public policies that were varied in time. These different variations can be used to draw up the typology of public policies.

The typologies of policies most used have been drawn up in the 1970s [9]. They combine two dimensions: the instruments of public action and the recipients. They are available through two parameters: the type of national (individual or collective) and the type of constraint (direct or indirect). The pooling of dimensions and parameters allows to distinguish four typologies of public policy:

- Regulatory policies that target individuals by means of a direct constraint. They consist to enact mandatory rules which apply to any individual in a given situation.

- The allocative policies which target individuals by means of an indirect constraint. They are based on the allocation of permissions or specific benefits.

		Constraint	
		Direct	**Indirect**
Public	Individual	Regulatory policy	Allocative policy
	Group	Redistributive policy	Constituent policy

Source: Ref. [9].

Table 1.
Typologies of public policy.

- Redistributive policies which aim groups of individuals by means of a direct constraint. They operate transfers between groups, often in a logic of solidarity.
- The procedural policies which aim groups of individuals by means of an indirect constraint. They lay down rules or procedures to follow that must respect the actors of public policies (**Table 1**).

2.3 Decentralized territorial communities and link of the implementation of public policies

Public policies are defined at the national level by the competent authorities, legislature and government, but they need a local anchor to realize that any policy could not be that territorialized. This "territorialization" is also done well with the services of the state at the local level than with the territorial communities. In fact, a unitary state cannot happen, our days, of a certain degree of decentralization. As well, the unitary decentralized state implies an association of territorial communities in the formulation of public policies decided at the national level.

2.3.1 The criteria for the characterization of the decentralized territorial communities

The territorial communities are separate administrative structures of the administration of the state, which must support the interests of the population of a specific territory. According to the territorial extent, three types of community can be identified: the commons, departments, and regions. Whatever the type, three criteria are essential in the definition of territorial communities:

- The moral personality, which enables him to act in justice. Allied to the decentralization, he makes the benefits for the territorial community of the administrative autonomy. It has its own personnel and its own budget.
- The specific skills, which are entrusted to it by the legislator (parliament). A territorial community is not a state within the state. It does not hold sovereignty and cannot acquire, its sole initiative, new bodies.
- The power of decision, by deliberation within a council of elected representatives. Decisions are then implemented by the executive power's premises.

However, the territorial communities do not follow all the same rules of operation and do not have the same status.

2.3.2 The means of control of the public policies of the decentralized territorial communities

The political actors, like the decentralized territorial communities, use public policies as a means of control, to their advantage, for decisions adopted for the regulation of public affairs. The decisions matter to the political actors because they relate to their resources [10]. Furthermore, the power is shown by the capacity of the political actors to limit the scope of the decision to which does not threaten their resources [11].

The resources, thus, constitute a means of control in the implementation of public policies. A categorization of resources can be made in the functions of the various strengths available in a territorial community to make its effective preferences about the various issues of public policy. The literature allows to highlight seven categories of resources:

- The normative resources, which correspond to the set of rules and values that the political actors use to serve as assets or that they seek to control the issues.

- The statutory resources, which refer to official or actual positions occupied by the actors. They constitute for the latter means of power.

- The action resources, which consist the levers of actions among the recipients of control.

- The relational resources, which refer to the links established with other actors.

- The hardware resources that make reference to the material and financial resources.

- The human resources that return to the workforce which has a political actor.

- The informational resources, which refer to information that has a political actor and that it can use to influence public policy.

The resources, thus, appear as instruments of public policy; they can be enabling for some actors and binding for others.

This section will be allowed to review the concept of public policy. They can be presented as recurrent attempts of regulation of public affairs by actors who seek to control decisions on the occasion of the process of formulation or implementation. The process of monitoring of policies by some actors, like the decentralized territorial communities, gives rise on the basis of the resources available and of power relations with other actors. The following section will illustrate the relationship of the decentralized territorial communities in the implementation of public policies in Cameroon.

3. Places of the decentralized territorial communities in Cameroon in the implementation of public policies

Invoking the decentralized territorial communities in fact appeals to the decentralization policy implementation in a country. For the specific case of Cameroon, the decentralization process has been recognized as a pillar of the socioeconomic development in the Constitution of 18 January 1996 [12]. This section will review the tasks assigned to the decentralization and the profile of the territorial communities as well as their missions and the state of things.

3.1 Decentralization according to the Cameroonian context

The constitutional revision of 18 January 1996 defines the legal regime and sets out the general principles of the decentralization in Cameroon. Also, Cameroon is a unitary state and decentralized. The law of orientation of the decentralization promulgated on 22 July 2004 is clarified in the institutional context of decentralization in Cameroon. In its second article, it defines the decentralization as a transfer by the state to the decentralized territorial communities of particular skills and appropriate means; this transfer obeys the principles of subsidiarity, progressivity, and complementarity [13].

For the Cameroonian legislature, decentralization must constitute the fundamental axis of promotion of development, democracy, and good governance at the local level. In the specific, it is question:

- In the area of promotion of local development: the achievement (increase, improvement) of basic social infrastructure. It also induces the improvement of incomes of the population at the base, thanks in particular to the promotion and financing of income-generating activities, for an improvement in the quality of life of populations and of their being.

- In regard to the strengthening of local democracy: the designation, either by consensus or by vote, by local populations of their representatives in the decision-making bodies.

- With regard to the promotion of good governance at the local level: the organization and functioning of communities through the exercise of power and the involvement of all the local actors (NGOs, organizations at the base, local population, etc.). The control of the local administration in the community of the inhabitants of the community is a pledge of the local governance [14].

3.2 The decentralized territorial communities in Cameroon: profile and responsibilities

The decentralized communities are defined as legal persons of public law, enjoying administrative and financial autonomy for the management of regional and local interests. The constitutional revision of 18 January 1996 defines two main decentralized communities: the regions and communes.

The commune is an old entity of the decentralization process in Cameroon initiated since 1974. The reforms of 2004 applicable to the commons specify the mission of the commons in the decentralization process. Those are the basic local communities which it returns the competence to manage local affairs under the guardianship of the state, in view of the social and cultural development of its people [15].

The region is the entity newly instituted by the Constitution of 1996. The reform of 2004 [16] devotes the missions identical to those of the commons. The only difference lies in the territorial coverage of the actions. The activities of the regions extend over the whole of the commons of its territorial jurisdiction which is not the case for the common whose activities do not limit that has its territory.

The territorial communities are involved in virtually all areas of the life of the populations: social, economic, health, and education. The specific responsibilities of each community in the different areas are reflected in **Table 2**.

		Responsibilities	
		The regions	**The commons**
Areas	Social and health policy	• Promote the hygiene and safety as well as the measures for the prevention of diseases • Organize and manage the supply of drugs and other health products • Participate in the development of the health map of the region; create, equip, manage, and maintain the infrastructure of health • Support the health infrastructure that exists • Maintain and manage the training centers and social reintegration • Organize and manage the assistance to needy layers • List the infrastructure of vocational training as well as the trades creation and maintenance of rural roads not classified, as well as the construction and management of trays of the crossing	• Provide support to the maintenance and management of the centers for promotion and social reintegration • Prepare the acts of civil status (copy and extract of the act of birth, marriage act, act of death) • Create, equip, manage, and maintain the health centers • Support the training of health and social issues that exist • Make quality controls in the structures of production, packaging, storage, and distribution of food entering the power supply of the populations • Ensure drinking water supply in areas not covered by the public network for the distribution of the water
	Economique	• Move the contracts/plans for the achievement of the objectives of development in partnership of the state • Promote small- and medium-sized enterprises (SMES) • Organize fairs and exhibitions • Promote the crafts and the agropastoral activities • Promote the regional associations of economic operators • Promote the tourism • Promote microprojects, revenue generators, and creators of jobs • Protect, maintain and manage the natural sites • Combat nuisance and pollution of waters; Create wood and protected areas • Emergency planning and the prevention of risks • Develop and execute plans for regional development • Organize and manage the intercity public transport	• Promote the agropastoral activities, fishery, and crafts • Create, develop, and maintain tourist sites • Build, equip, manage, and maintain markets, stations road, and abattoirs • Plan and execute the communal investments • Monitor and control the management of industrial waste, as well as the garbage • Combat nuisance and pollution, including pollution of surface water and groundwater • Ensure the hygiene and the safety of public places • Plan and monitor the activities for the protection of the environment • Improve access to drinking water • Organize and manage exhibitions of a commercial character • Promote and support the microprojects generators of revenue and creators of jobs

	Responsibilities	
	The regions	**The commons**
	• Develop the regional plan of development of the territory • Coordinate the actions of development • Support the plans and actions of communal urbanization and habitat	• Establish industrial zones • Manage, in partnership with the State and the region, the contracts and the plans of the commune in order to achieve the objectives of development • Plan and control the occupation of land by issuing the building permit, to subdivide, demolish and implement • Create, maintain the municipal roads and develop the related activities relating thereto • Develop and servicing the habitable space • Name and address the streets, buildings and public spaces
Cultural life	• Create, equip, manage, and maintain the high schools and public colleges • Recruit staff for these schools • Participate in the development of the school map of the region • Distribute and allocate aid and school grants • Support the commons for the acquisition of textbooks, school supplies, and teaching materials for training centers • Develop the school map related to technical and vocational education as well as the plans for the professional insertion of young people • Promote the partnership schools-companies • Promote, organize, and manage the sports activities • Put in place the infrastructure and equipment for the promotion of local cultures	• Create, equip, manage, and maintain schools, nursery, primary, and preschool • Recruit staff for these schools • Provide support to the management and administration of the schools • Support the creation and maintenance of the educational infrastructure and training centers • Plan the insertion and the professional reintegration of young people • Promote and animate sports activities and the youth • Create and manage municipal stages, swimming pools, sports courses, the areas of games, and the arenas • Organize days and cultural events, traditional, literary and artistic works with competition • Support the cultural associations; in partnership with the region, promoting the national languages

Source: Authors.

Table 2.
Responsibilities of the municipalities and regions in the framework of decentralization in Cameroon.

The reading of the legal framework and regulatory governing the decentralized territorial communities in Cameroon allows to raise that they have three essential criteria, namely, the moral personality, the specific skills, and the power of decision. It remains only to examine the effectiveness of the resources of those communities for the implementation of public policies.

3.3 State of the availability of resources of the decentralized territorial communities of Cameroon for an implementation of optimal public policies

The text of law on the orientation of the decentralization stipulates that the state should transfer to the communities the skills and appropriate means. This transfer is in reality the resources granted to them for the implementation of public policies at the local level. The state of the resources available to the communities is presented on the financial plan, human, statutory, physical, and normative.

3.3.1 State of financial resources

Financial resources should give local and regional authorities financial autonomy. This is also the basis for the transfer of financial resources by the state to local authorities. Cameroonian municipalities manage three types of resources:

- Own resources derived from activities carried out on their territory
- Resources from the treasury
- Resources obtained within the framework of decentralized cooperation (although these are now "managed by the state")

However, the financial autonomy of local authorities is relative because of the following legal provisions:

- Equalization, which is the obvious manifestation of the guardianship's intervention in local management
- Levying of 10% of the additional municipal fees by the state, which reduces the self-financing capacity of local authorities and, thus, compromises local development
- The power granted to the prefect to correct an unbalanced budget
- The financial controller's approval of any financial act by local authorities

It should be noted that according to the legal provisions [17], "authorizing officers are required to produce an administrative account showing the acts of their management and a performance report on programmes and projects." But only the approximate knowledge of the budgetary procedure by many municipal authorities leads them to budget deviations that are difficult to justify and to a low mobilization of their own resources, which are nevertheless necessary for the smooth running of services and the inclusive development of the commune. They would find it very difficult to produce their management account [18].

3.3.2 Normative resources

The normative resources are the bedrock of the administrative autonomy devolved to territorial communities by the legislator. However, the reading of the legal provisions and the observation of current practices allow raising the limits:

- All deliberations of the territorial communities must be approved by the tutorship.

- The guardianship may suspend the municipal council, the dissolve.
- The mayor can be suspended by the guardianship.

3.3.3 Statutory resources

The statutory resources refer to the operational organization and function of the territorial community. In practice, each organization should put to a specific position a person who can have control. In the framework of territorial communities in Cameroon, some employees are designated by the central administration:

- The secretary-general of the town hall who is a servant placed at the disposal of the municipality by the department in charge of the decentralization and deals with the mayor in a relationship of a horizontal collaboration: he is not his subordinate.
- The municipal tax collector who is an official of the ministry in charge of finance, which deals with the authorizing officer in a relationship of collaboration: he is not his subordinate and has no orders to receive from him.
- The delegate of the government who is an agent appointed by the state and has more weight than the elected representatives of the people that are the mayors.

3.3.4 Human resources

The organic framework on decentralization provides that the territorial communities recruit and manage freely their human resources. However, some officials of the communities, as seen by examining the statutory resources, are appointed by the central administration. In addition to this, there is a tendency to neglect the recruitment of staff in particular with regard to the adequacy profile/employment and a lack of the texts of application on the local public service.

3.3.5 Hardware resources

The limited nature of the financial resources available to the territorial communities is borne from their staffing in materials and equipment to fully play their role in the implementation of public policies. The case visible enough is that of the development of communal roads or the equipment of communal health centers. This state of things can be explained by the absence of a regulatory framework on the devolution to the commons of material means corresponding to the block of skills already transferred.

The review of the status of the resources available to the decentralized territorial communities allows to raise that these actors of public policies do not have real means of decisions on the implementation of public policies in Cameroon. In effect, the National Council of Decentralization noted that local development is still mixed in Cameroon and this is despite the advances made in the transfer of skills and resources in the House of Commons since 2010 [19]. Also, this local development remains focused essentially on the political and social dimensions and the detriment of the economic dimension.

4. Conclusion

The objective of this article was to gauge the weight of decentralized local authorities in the implementation of public policies in Cameroon and thus to assess the effectiveness of decentralization. The result was a mixed weight of decentralization on the local development front. This reflects the efforts required for local authorities to be genuinely involved in the formulation and implementation of local public policies.

Decentralization is not an innovation in Cameroon, but related practices do not always follow the existing legal framework. It is not enough just here to want but to give power and let the local authorities act. The state would come after to control and not to rule. Indeed, decentralized local authorities will only play their part perfectly if the strategic state/CTD partnership is backed by a clear legal and regulatory framework, lending little to variable geometric interpretations, and if the state improves its strategy for managing its triple function of the strategic state (facilitator, regulator, and developer).

On the normative level, the legal arsenal in Cameroon is well provided in terms of decentralization, and its implementation is necessary to achieve local development objectives. Its operationalization is manifested by the transfer of skills in several fields that are the social, economic, and cultural. However, a relevant analysis of the legal framework and the mechanisms for setting up effective decentralization in Cameroon shows that in reality, as things stand, local authorities have no financial autonomy and have very limited administrative autonomy. Beyond the technical capacities that they do not yet have, we note the weight of supervision that weighs on those responsible at the local level. The existence of so many shortcomings attests that decentralized local authorities are not always provided with adequate local services and personnel for the optimal exercise of their competences. This assessment is the marker of an administrative autonomy of the communes still fragile to serve as a basis for local development.

On the financial level, given that state allocations are largely insufficient to enable local authorities to develop, only local taxes can play a determining role in their financial empowerment. Public authorities should, therefore, review the distribution of local tax revenues in such a way that local authorities are able to finance themselves and reduce financial intermediation as regards the financial circuit of local taxes. One strategy could initially be to reduce the procedures for making financial resources available to local authorities and to strengthen the mechanism for monitoring the implementation by the latter of their program budgets.

In statutory terms, the legitimacy of government delegates should be guaranteed. Therefore, they should be chosen by municipal councilors from among elected mayors who demonstrate the will to assume these functions. Moreover, the state should put in place a strategy that would ensure that, in the long term, the municipal council can be the only body that controls the mayor's action at the local level and effectively plays the role that the National Assembly plays alongside the executive at the national level. Also, the municipal receiver and the mayor's secretary should be placed under the authority of the mayor in a vertical collaborative relationship in order to limit confrontations between these officials in matters of local management.

Author details

Guy Yakana Yombi*, Mounton Chouaïbou and Lucie Yakana Agoume
Univerité of Yaoundé, SOA, Cameroon

*Address all correspondence to: Guyyakana@yahoo.com

References

[1] Dye TR. Party and policy in the States. The Journal of Politics. 1984; **46**(4):1097-1116

[2] Sharkansky I. Policy Analysis in Political Science. Markham Pub. Co; 1970

[3] Bellavance M. The quebecois clergy and the Canadian Confederation in 1867 [Doctoral thesis]; 1985

[4] Jenkins WI. Policy Analysis: A Political and Organizational Perspective. London: Mr. Robertson; 1978

[5] Rakoff SH, Schaefer GF. Politics, policy, and political science: Theoretical alternatives. Politics and Society. 1970; **1**(1):51-77

[6] Anderson MH. Madison Avenue in Asia: Politics and Transnational Advertising. Fairleigh Dickinson Univ Press; 1984

[7] Pal LA. The political executive and political leadership in Alberta. Government and Politics in Alberta. 1992:1-29

[8] Kaplan A. Power and Society: A Framework for Political Inquiry. New Haven: Yale University Press; 1950

[9] Lowi TJ. Four systems of policy, politics, and choice. Public Administration Review. 1972;**32**(4): 298-310

[10] Lemieux V. The Québec Public Administration: Sectoral Developments, 1960–1985. Bélanger Yves and Lepage Laurent (under the direction of) Sillery: The Presses of the University of Quebec; 1989. 226 p. Canadian Journal of Political Science. 1990;**23**(3):562-564

[11] Bachrach P, Baratz MS. Power and Poverty: Theory and Practice. Oxford University Press; 1970

[12] Act No. 96/06 of 18 January 1996 on the Revision of the Constitution of 02 June 1972 in the Republic of Cameroon

[13] Act No. 2004-17 of 22 July 2004 in the Orientation of Decentralization in the Republic of Cameroon

[14] Mback CN. Decentralization in Africa: Issues and Prospects. Contemporary Africa; 2001. pp. 95-114

[15] Act No. 2004/018 of 22 July 2004 Laying Down the Rules Applicable to the House of Commons in the Republic of Cameroon

[16] Act No. 2004/019 of 22 July 2004 Laying Down the Rules Applicable to the Regions in the Republic of Cameroon

[17] Act No. 2009/011 of 10 July 2009 on the Financial Regime of Decentralized Territorial Authorities in the Republic of Cameroon

[18] CAMERCAP-PARC Study with a View to Improving the Contribution of Decentralized Territorial Communities to Growth Through the Supply of Available Factors of Production; 2018

[19] National Council of Decentralization. Final Report of the Impact Evaluation Study of the Decentralization Policy on the Cameroonian populations since 2010; 2016

Chapter 5

Financial Relationships Between Public Administration and Public Enterprises: Theoretical Foundations and Practical Implications

Pina Puntillo

Abstract

The objective of this study is to analyze the institutional and organizational structure of public service companies in Italy. After analyzing the various reforms of the Public Administration, research has focused on the crisis and the insolvency of publicly owned companies, as, for the first time and recently the legislator has organically regulated the consequences of the insolvency of the same, affirming their general submission to bankruptcy and insolvency proceedings. Still the norm also outlined the procedure for the adoption of preventive plans should aim to avoid insolvency in financial hardship cases, and to remedy the crisis of the investee companies. After having dealt with the issue of historical evolution and territorial distribution of the phenomenon of public enterprises in Italy, aspects of the legal framework of the object of study will be addressed. The next section analyzes the contents of the reform of public companies, recalling the reference standards and the important news concerning the coverage of losses of companies. The new discipline produces important repercussions on public budgets and therefore on the community: for this reason, the conclusions of the study will deal with this aspect.

Keywords: public service companies, default, budget, Italy

1. Introduction

The objective of this study is to analyze the institutional and organizational structure of public service companies in Italy. This structure was the subject of a profound reform generated by reasons of public finance protection. After analyzing the concept of the public sector and the object of this study, the theoretical framework of the analysis will be addressed, which will be carried out from a historical-temporal perspective, with an interpretation of a company nature on observation phenomena.

In this sense, recalling what is reported in national and international literature, we analyzed the different strands of research that characterized the various reforms of the public administration. Research areas have shifted the objectives of the studies toward conditions of greater efficiency and value of public performance while allowing to identify and analyze the evolution of the various systems of planning and control of public administration. In consideration of the pathological phenomena that have occurred with increasing frequency in recent years, research has focused on the crisis and the insolvency of publicly owned companies, as, for the first time and recently the legislator has organically regulated the consequences of the insolvency of the same, affirming their general submission to bankruptcy and insolvency proceedings. Still the norm also outlined the procedure for the adoption of preventive plans should aim to avoid insolvency in financial hardship cases and to remedy the crisis of the investee companies. After having dealt with the issue of historical evolution and territorial distribution of the phenomenon of public enterprises in Italy, aspects of the legal framework of the object of study will be addressed. This last topic is very controversial in doctrine; in fact, far from being a mere academic exercise, the qualification of the legal nature of such enterprises involves significant practical consequences on the *disciplinary* level. The next section analyzes the contents of the reform of public companies, recalling the reference standards and the important news concerning the coverage of losses of companies. The new discipline produces important repercussions on public budgets and therefore on the community: for this reason the conclusions of the study will deal with this aspect.

2. What constitutes the public sector and the public entities: defining boundaries

The public sector is traditionally constituted by all organizations owned and controlled by government, which provide utilities and services to the community [1].

Especially public complex and difficult to define, inputs are not being easily measured, and as a consequence, it is difficult to value the public sector efficiency [2].

Public entities differ from private sector organizations, but rather the delivery of outcomes to stakeholders [3].

Bossi et al. [4] have identified specific characteristics that define the public sector in relation to the private sector:

- Less incentive to adopt new management approaches, due to a non-competitive environment.
- Intangible objectives are less linked with the market value and financial profit.
- More importance is given to social and environmental responsibility.
- Most public organizations provide services (education, health, etc.), that is, intangibles.
- Intangibles—knowledge and human resources.
- Inflexible management procedures and rigid structures—the bureaucratic model does not facilitate new approaches.
- Less necessity to quantify.
- Increase in external demand for accountability and transparency in the use of public funds.

In general terms, we can point out that the public sector has experienced great processes of intense transformation which have been caused mainly by two factors: (1) financial and tax burdens, and as a result, the increasing importance of an efficient public sector management and (2) society's new demands to improve services [5].

The modern public sector management boasts public attention and service quality, which justifies the need to establish a series of initiatives to help efficiency and effectiveness in the public function.

The concepts related to innovation in the public sector can be included in new managerial view (or framework) of governmental administration called new public management (NPM) [6] since public service quality improves.

According to the paradigm of NPM, the role of public entities is changed to the name of decentralization, increase in autonomy of public managers, competition, quality strategies, economy, efficiency and efficacy, citizen guidance, emphasis on private sector management techniques, and performance indicators.

Since the new vision of public administration is the result of a process for the introduction of the principles of NPM [7–9].

NPM has brought about transformations in managing entities in public entities, whose main characteristics—defined by Hood [10], Olsen and Peters [11], and Hodges and Mellet [8]—include a wide variety of changes such as deregulation, decentralization, subcontracting, substitution of input control systems, management of results, responsibility assignment, and the introduction of different management techniques. The ultimate objective of these reforms is to improve the efficacy and effectiveness of public entities, surpassing bureaucratic problems and guaranteeing transparency in entities and accounts renderings.

As a result of NPM, public entities better response to the needs of service users, emphasis on performance and result management, introduction of performance standards, better communication of results, decentralization and competence of financial and personal management, interest in market forces and the creation of internal markets, privatization of public companies, and application of private sector management methods [12].

These characteristics all justify the need to draw together in an easily understandable system to those elements that are differentiating the sources of competition and that will generate value for the administration, such as the focus on the citizen, social responsibility, and professionalism.

In order to achieve this task, we consider public funding, ownership and operation of services. These organizations may be part of two areas of activity: the other is those monopolies which supply services and utilities and which also charge their customers for their services. In the 1990, the policy of privatization has made it more difficult the identification of public sector, given the less direct links which now exist between organizations and government.

The provision of public services may be organized in a variety of ways and controls through different organizational and regulatory mechanisms. Public services might have some element of government funding, ownership, public direction, or regulation, in different combinations, but there is no longer a need for direct government ownership for the provision of these public services. This study includes some hybrid organizations, in which private sectors were used by the public sector and public service organizations were urgent to be "commercial."

Public services are those activities that are enshrined within the public service rather than the private provision through market. It is assumed these "public services" should be available for all members of the society provided in an equitable fashion [1].

Regime around it is a complex of domains of public services that relies on the perceived nature of the services. This is for several reasons. The main issue concerns the nature of public services and is widely used by the public services to be provided, that is, the boundary of public services is not fixed but varies from country to country. Thus, we use only the public services business (PBE) but not public institutional systems (PIS).

In light of this premise, the research field identifies which universe of companies on which the investigation is to be carried out partially or totally held directly or indirectly by public administrations, with the following legal form:

- Srl and SpA
- Srl and SpA in cooperative form
- Consortium companies in the form of Srl or SpA

3. Public companies in Italy: evolutionary profiles

The reasons behind the latest reform of publicly owned companies are the need to simplify and rationalize an impressive number of public companies in Italy.

For the purposes of the analysis of the regulations contained in Legislative Decree 175/2016 laying down "*Consolidated Law on the subject of companies owned by the public administration,*" it is necessary to define a public entity, and therefore, it is necessary to start from the models of public bodies that have become known over time.

The administrative organization of *the liberal state* was simple and was characterized by few territorial entities: state, provinces, and municipalities. There were, also, very few other government-owned businesses by local authorities, who mostly were characterized by a structure-associated ativa.

This state was essentially concerned with controlling the internal public order and the defense of the territory from external enemies, leaving the market free to seek its equilibrium.

Toward the end of the nineteenth century and the beginning of the twentieth century, the state was strengthened, with the relative growth of the ministries and agencies that began to take care of public services.

This historical moment marks the start of the process of expansion of the original organizational structures of the state, with the creation, at the state level, of *autonomous companies* (entities included in the ministerial area with management autonomy and a different financial, accounting and controls), while at the local level, *municipalized companies* (as branches of the territorial bodies that carried out, at the levels closest to the citizen, the same functions of the autonomous companies), as well as with the multiplication of functional public bodies, which has led to a progressive differentiation and multiplication of public bodies. We pass, in this way, from one State controller to an "*interventionist*."

Following the crisis of 1929, as well as in the post-war period, there was a strong state intervention in the economy due to the consequential economic difficulties of these historical events.

In particular, the state started to take stock of private companies in difficulty in order to avoid bankruptcy (e.g., the purchase of shareholdings by IRI, an institute for industrial reconstruction).

We have thus moved on to a model of State *entrepreneur* and lender.

With the entry into force of the Constitution, the panorama of public bodies has been enriched by another body: the region (public body endowed with legislative and statutory power in certain matters listed in Article 117 of the Constitution) and with the reform of the Title V administrative functions has been redistributed with a view to subsidiarity, differentiation, and adequacy.

In the same perspective of the evolution of the group of public subjects, the law on parastato (L.70/1975) continued the work of transformation through an uncontrolled proliferation of necessary public bodies, qualified as parastatals. This framework has made it difficult to give a single definition of public administration, or we speak, in fact, of *pluralism of public administrations* or *public administrations with variable geometry*.

This organizational pluralism is presented as:

- Pluralism of public authority (state, regions, and local authorities)
- Pluralism of the state organization (plurality of ministries)
- Plurality of public bodies (i.e., organizations differentiated by public authorities in the strict sense and endowed with their own legal personality but linked to them by more or less intense organizational ties)

Uniformity has given way to the diversification of models, envisaging a system of administration no longer revolving around the State-apparatus, but inspired by the principle of institutional pluralism, by virtue of which alongside the State, the public body par excellence and other subjects operate and are endowed, as well as of private juridical capacity, also of public juridical capacity, which pursue aims of public interest.

Figure 1.
Public companies currently controlled by the Ministry of the Economy and Finance.

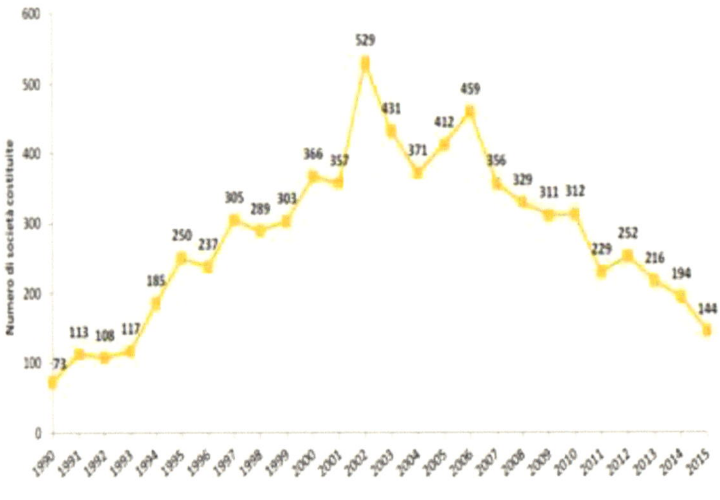

Figure 2.
Number of public enterprises by year of establishment from 1990 to 2015.

The penetrating intervention of the State in the economy has led to an uncontrollable increase in public debt, imposing a peculiar process of liberalization and privatization in order to reduce it. **Figures 1** and **2** show a quantitative analysis of the public investee companies in Italy, illustrating the public companies currently controlled by the Ministry of the Economy and Finance and the number of public companies established between 1990 and 2015.

4. Legal profiles and disciplinary aspects of public enterprises

With the privatization process, there have arisen problems of formal classification of the discipline; in fact, within the syntagma "public companies" can be, in practice, surrounded by deeply heterogeneous figures. It is for this reason that it cannot be further supported by a static concept of a public body, indeed, must give notice of the fact that recently the Stato Council (judgment no. 2660/2015[1]) is oriented toward a "functional and iridescent notion of public body: the same subject may have the nature of public body for certain purposes and with respect to certain institutions and may, however, not have it for other purposes, preserving, respect to other institutions, and regulatory regimes of a private nature."

Far from being a merely classificatory matter, the public qualification of an institution involves significant practical consequences on the *disciplinary* level.

A first limit is found in the controls, of various kinds (on the deeds, on the management bodies, internal or external, accounting), which are the object of all public bodies, aimed at assessing the legitimacy of the institution's activity and compliance in the public interest.

A strong limitation is, moreover, by the absence of a complete and perfect negotiating freedom, characterized by a number of constraints, rules, and publicistic limits, aimed at transparent proceduralisation of a contractual choice, with regard to *an,* the content of the contract and the choice of the negotiating partner. It is

[1] https://www.giustizia-amministrativa.it/cdsintra/cdsintra/AmministrazionePortale/DocumentViewer/index.html?ddocname=7CQIJE5IDUT64IMHJ4XI75AXDE&q.

therefore an activity that is always functional and not free, characterized, that is, by a teleological constraint susceptible of control and syndication in the jurisdictional seat.

With regard to the configurability of public bodies to a corporate structure, the debate has polarized around the question of whether the public finalization of the corporate body and the alteration of the typical corporate model can lead to affirming the attraction of the so-called investee companies to the public sphere.

This assimilation took place fundamentally for reasons of public finance protection, given that often the private module constitutes an elusive means of provisions that are undoubtedly binding on the (public) participating bodies but not also for the private entities constituted or participated by them. In general, it should be noted that nowadays there is a tendency to identify between public bodies and institutions included in the consolidated account of the public administration.

The growing attention on the system of public investments, at central and territorial level, is a consequence of the previous use of the corporate instrument as a way of avoiding the constraints of public finance. In compliance with the new rules on budget balances, the legislator has set up a coherent system of measures, directed toward the common objective of restoring efficiency to companies in public participation, including through the strengthening of corporate governance and to consider the "public administration group" (GAP) in a unified manner, with particular reference to the effects on institutions of the results of the exercise of the investee organizations.

The lack of homogeneity of the financial statements, determined by the phenomenon of outsourcing, involved an incomplete and not representative representation of the financial, economic, and equity situation of the GAP and the overall functions performed by the entity through its organizational structures, its instrumental entities, and its investee companies.

With a view to greater transparency and accountability of the various levels of government, Legislative Decree June 23, 2011, n. 118, in harmonizing the accounting systems and financial statements of the regions, provinces, and local authorities, establishes the consolidation of the accounts between the institutions and their participated bodies.

The "centrality of the consolidated financial statements" is functional to compliance with the public finance constraints, since it allows to achieve the objective of "neutrality" of the budget with respect to the phenomenon of outsourcing and is approved by 30 September of the year following the reference year (accounting principle applied consolidated financial statements). The scope of consolidation extends to cases in which the dominant influence is exercised by virtue of particular contractual restrictions, even in the absence of participation. The obligation of consolidation, long postponed, from September 30, 2017, is mandatory for all institutions with a population of more than 5000 inhabitants. In force since 2018, the financial statements that present, for each of the three parameters (total assets, net assets, and total revenues), are less than 3% compared to the parent company's economic and financial position.

The valuation of irrelevance must be formulated both with reference to the single entity or company and to the set of entities and companies considered to be scarcely significant, as the consideration of more modest situations could be of interest for consolidation purposes. It must be avoided that the exclusion of so many autonomously insignificant realities subtracts important information from the group budget. Consider, for example, the limit case of a corporate group consisting of a considerable number of institutions and companies, all of a small size such as to allow exclusion if considered individually.

Therefore, for the purposes of exclusion for irrelevance, starting from the financial year 2018, the sum of the percentages of the financial statements considered as irrelevant must present, for each of the parameters indicated above, an incidence of less than 10% compared to the equity, economic, and financial management of the parent company. If these sums have a value equal to or greater than 10%, the parent company identifies the financial statements of the individually irrelevant entities to be included in the consolidated financial statements, until the sum of the percentages of the accounts excluded for irrelevance is reduced to less than 10%.

On the other hand, the entities and companies wholly owned by the parent company and the *in-house* companies and the investee entities holding direct assignment by the members of the group, irrespective of the shareholding, are considered significant.

In the case of direct assignment, the shareholdings of less than 1% of the investee company's capital are considered irrelevant and not subject to consolidation.

The amplitude of the scope of consolidation makes it possible to achieve a unitary economic result of the "public administration group," which takes into account both the result of the institution's exercise and the profits and losses of the investee organizations.

The proliferation of participating companies is now a phenomenon subject to attention by the Court of Auditors, which has identified the critical profiles of the use of the corporate instrument for the pursuit of the institutional goals of public bodies. The Autonomous Section of the Court of Auditors[2] in resolution no. 24/2015 highlighted the fact that only 35.72% of the participated bodies operate in the local public services sector, with a clear predominance of *in-house* assignments *with* respect to assignments through public tenders. From the point of view of financial management, the Court of Auditors highlighted the strong prevalence of debts on loans in the relations between local authorities and investee companies.

The regulatory framework, in the field of public companies, presented a strong regulatory disorder that negatively characterized the regulation of corporate holdings held by public administrations.

In consideration of this, it was necessary to introduce a unitary discipline aimed at resolving the classification problems and legal regime of these subjects.

It is for this reason that the Parliament, with the law of August 7, 2015, has delegated the government to adopt a decree reforming the public administration as a whole.

The purpose of the reform, as stated by the Council of State in its opinion no. 968/2016[3], is to "*simplify and rationalize the rules in force in this area, through the reorganization of national provisions and the creation of an organic general discipline*."

5. The reform of public enterprises as an instrument for rationalizing public spending in Italy

These are the essential points of the intervention delegated by the Madia reform:

- Firstly, limit the establishment of new public companies, make the financial statements of companies in public control transparent, reduce the number of public companies, and prevent the proliferation of unnecessary societies.

[2] http://www.corteconti.it/export/sites/portalecdc/_documenti/controllo/sez_autonomie/2015/20150720_20150722_Deln024_FRG_Organismi_Partecipati_Linkrelto.pdf.

[3] https://www.giustizia-amministrativa.it/cdsintra/cdsintra/Notiziasingola/Ilcodicedeicontratti pubblici/PareriresidalConsigliodiStato/Parere21aprile2016968/index.html.

- Secondly, reduce the areas of intervention of public companies, eliminate or limit public companies that are not in economic equilibrium, redefine the personnel management system of publicly controlled companies, and ensure that the activities of publicly owned companies are more efficient.

- Finally, improve the services provided to citizens and businesses, giving greater credibility and transparency to the public administration and favoring the best use of public resources, through the efficient allocation of resources and the removal of waste sources.

This is the framework in which the Legislative Decree 175/2016 laying down "Consolidated Law on the subject of companies owned by the public administration," then amended by Legislative Decree, 100/2017.

The Consolidation Act is essentially divided into four types of intervention:

- Introductory provisions containing the indication of the object and scope of the TU, the formulation of definitions, and the identification of the types of companies in which public participation is admitted

- Provisions aimed at establishing the conditions and limits of public shareholdings, as well as redefining the rules for the incorporation of companies or for the taking up or maintenance of shareholdings by public authorities and for the sale of public holdings

- Provisions concerning the administrative and control bodies of publicly controlled companies

- Provisions aimed at encouraging economic efficiency and efficiency through the introduction of procedures for periodic rationalization and extraordinary auditing, personnel management, specific financial rules for the local authorities' subsidiaries and the promotion of transparency

The Consolidation Act draws the "perimeter" within which a public administration can decide to set up a company (in the forms, governed by the Civil Code, of joint-stock companies or limited liability companies), specifying in Art. 4, paragraph 1, that "le Public administrations cannot directly or indirectly constitute companies having as their object activities of production of goods and services not strictly necessary for the pursuit of its institutional purposes or acquire or to maintain holdings, including minorities, in these companies."

This is the so-called **restriction of purpose,** drawn up by the jurisprudence and implemented by the delegated legislator, which places a limit on the participation of the public administration in companies, so that they pursue a purpose compatible with the institutional purpose of the participating administration.

Paragraph 2, of the Art. 4, also introduces an **activity constraint**: companies in which public administrations can participate and perform "exclusively" certain activities, strictly listed (e.g., production of a service of general interest, design and construction of a work published on the basis of a program agreement, self-production of goods or services instrumental to the participating institution or public bodies, etc.).

The most important aspects of Legislative Decree 175/2016 then amended by the Legislative Decree, 100/2017, are essentially concern with:

- Art 20–24 rationalization plans
- Art 14 recapitalization
- Art 21 financial rules

The main instrument through which the need to reduce public spending has been pursued is the obligation to periodically rationalize public holdings, to which the administrations are held annually.

The rationalization plans concern all public administrations and are designed to highlight the following situations:

a. Company shareholdings that are not included among those "indispensables" for the purposes of pursuing institutional goals.

b. Companies that do not have employees or have more directors than employees.

c. Investments in companies that perform similar activities to those carried out by other investee companies or by instrumental public bodies (the so-called dual company).

d. Investments in companies which, in the previous 3 years, have achieved an average turnover not exceeding 1 million euro[4].

e. Investments in companies other than those established for the management of a service of general interest that has produced a negative result for four of the previous 5 years.

f. Investments in companies with a need to contain operating costs.

g. Investments in companies that need to be aggregated regarding the activities permitted pursuant to Art. 4 (see Article 20, paragraph 2).

The real novelty of the Consolidated Law consists in the provision of a periodic revision alongside the extraordinary one, providing that the public administrations carry out, annually (from 2018, by December 31) and the analysis of the investments held and prepare rationalization plans, according to the criteria enunciated by the aforementioned Art. 20.

To complete the reorganization procedure, the **Art. 24** of the disciplinary decree regulates the procedure for the extraordinary compulsory review of investments held, directly or indirectly, by public administrations, for the disposal or rationalization of certain types of companies.

The section of the autonomies, with resolution n. 19/SEZAUT/2017/INPR[5] issued guidelines aimed at favoring the correct fulfillment of the provisions,

[4] With the modification provided by the Art. 17, co. 1, lett. (f), Legislative Decree no. 100/2017, the turnover threshold, during the transition period, has been reduced to 500,000.00 euros. See Art. 26, co. 12-quinquies, Legislative Decree no. 175/2016: "For the purposes of applying the criterion referred to in Article 20, paragraph 2, letter (d), the first 3-year period is the 3-year period 2017–2019. Pending the first application of the aforementioned criterion for the 3-year period 2017–2019, the average turnover threshold not exceeding 500,000 euro applies for the 3 years preceding the entry into force of this decree for the purpose of adopting the extraordinary audit plans in Article 24 and for the 3-year periods 2015–2017 and 2016–2018 for the purposes of the adoption of the rationalization plans referred to in Article 20."

[5] http://www.corteconti.it/export/sites/portalecdc/_documenti/controllo/sez_autonomie/2017/delibera_19_sezaut_inpr_2017_e_linee_guida.pdf.

underlining the obligatory nature of the recognition of the investments held, so that the recognition is always necessary and also to certify the absence of shareholdings.

The rationalization plan includes:

- The recognition of holdings held.
- Decision of those not necessary for the pursuit of the corporate purpose.

The results of the survey are left to the discretion of the participating administrations, which are required to expressly motivate the choice made that may consist of a reorganization measure (alienation /rationalization/merger) and the maintenance of participation without intervention. In any case, a motivation is required, both for dismissing and for maintaining the company.

In summary, the aforementioned regulation provides two dismissal obligations:

a. The prohibition of maintaining companies that are not consistent with their institutional aims (principle of functionalization);

b. The prohibition to maintain companies, which are consistent with the institutional aims of the institution, are not indispensable for their prosecution (see Corte conti Lombardia Section control, resolution of May 13, 2015, No. 195; Corte conti-Basilicata Sez control, resolution of 14 June 2017, No. 40; Corte conti-Piemonte Control Section, Resolution No. 28 of January 28, 2016; and Court of Auditors-Emilia Romagna Control Section, Resolution 12 January 2016, No. 4).

6. The accounting tools for covering losses of public companies

Among the fundamental principles that characterize the accounting harmonization reform, there is the recourse to adequate allocations to specific provisions for risks and charges (in the past often hidden among the residual liabilities) destined to safeguard the present and future balance of the financial statements. With this in mind, the provision for the investee loss provision is envisaged, in addition to the tied multiyear fund and the doubtful loan fund.

First envisaged by Art. 1, cc. 550 et seq of Law 147/20 13 (2014 Stability Law) and, currently, governed by Art. 21, Legislative Decree no. 175/2016, the obligation is foreseen (which will come into force at full capacity from 2018 but provides for a transitional regime of first application already in the 3-year period 2015–2017) for local public administrations to set up a fixed fund to cover the losses of participated bodies not immediately cleared up.

The establishment of the captive fund to cover the losses of investee organizations will make it possible to include in the financial statements of local authorities the effects of losses incurred by these entities, and not immediately repaid. As emphasized by the Court[6], the fund:

- Avoids, in the forecast budget, that the failure to take into account any losses reported by the body could have a negative impact on future budget balances.

---

6 http://www.corteconti.it/export/sites/portalecdc/_documenti/controllo/campania/pareri/2016/delibera_333_2016.pdf.

- Favors the progressive managerial accountability of the member bodies, through a stringent correlation between the economic-financial dynamics of the investee organizations and those of the entrusting members.

The obligation to create the fixed fund for the losses of the participated bodies concerns all local public administrations included in the ISTAT list referred to in Article 1, paragraph 3 of Law 196/09. Therefore, in addition to regions, provinces, and municipalities, the provision calls into question, among others, mountain communities, unions of municipalities, consortia between local authorities, chambers of commerce, and local health authorities.

The "participatory bodies" that the Art. 1, c. 550[7] considers for the purpose of determining the provision to the fund are special companies, institutions, and investee companies. The financial intermediaries referred to Art. 106 of Legislative Decree 385/93 (Consolidated Law on Banking and Credit Law), as well as companies issuing financial instruments listed on regulated markets and their subsidiaries. It should also be noted that the provision is made if the investee organizations present, in the last available financial year, a financial result or a negative financial balance, not immediately paid by the participating entity (Article 1, paragraph 551).

Article 21 d. Legislative Decree 175/2016, as amended by Legislative Decree 100/2017, establishes that in the event that companies in which local public administrations have a negative operating result, the participating local public administrations, which adopt financial accounting, set aside subsequent year in an appropriate *restricted fund* an amount equal to the negative result, in proportion to the shareholding.

It should be noted that the Art. 21 of Legislative Decree. 175/2016 is also concerned with standardizing the cases in which the entities holding the loss-making interest are not in financial accounting but adopt a civil accounting system. In such cases, they adjust the value of the investment, during the following year, to the amount corresponding to the fraction of the equity of the investee company where the negative result is not immediately settled and constitutes a lasting loss in value.

For companies that prepare consolidated financial statements, the operating result to be considered is that relating to these financial statements.

The amount set aside returns to availability to the public administration budget, always in proportion to the participation fee, in the following cases:

- The participant body stores the loss or retires the participation.
- The participant is placed in liquidation.
- The investee companies, with their own resources, pay in full or in part the losses achieved in previous years.

Apart from these cases, the provision allocated to the budget is included in the statement of the share of the administrative result and therefore remains essentially unavailable for purposes of expenditure other than those for which it was established.

[7] Art. 1 c. 550 applies to special companies, institutions, and companies owned by local public administrations indicated in the list referred to in Art. 1, of Law 196/2009. Financial intermediaries pursuant to Art. 106 of the consolidated text referred to in d. lgs n. 385/1993, as well as companies issuing financial instruments listed on regulated markets and their subsidiaries.

In the first application, for the years 2015, 2016, and 2017, the legislator has provided a transitional period in which the provision is gradually increasing, with an important distinction between the participation in bodies that, despite having reported a loss in last available budget, the accounts worsened and those that improved them compared to the average of the previous 3 years.

The first situation includes the hypotheses of the bodies that recorded a loss after previous financial statements in profit or which reported a negative result above the average of the previous 3-year period. In these cases, the portion to be allocated in the 2015 financial statements of the participating entity is equal to 25% of the negative result achieved in the previous year by the body. The provisions will be set at 50% for 2016 and at 75% for 2017, again with reference to the losses reported by the investee in the previous year.

If, on the other hand, the loss in the last available balance sheet is lower than the average of the previous 3 years (showing an improvement in the accounts), the provision in the 2015 estimated budget must be made equal to the difference between the result achieved in previous year and the 2011–2013 average result improved by 25% for 2014. In the following financial years, the amount should be calculated as a slide considering that the average result must be improved by 50% for 2015 and by 75% for 2016.

The Autonomy Section of the Court of Auditors, which with Resolution no. 4 of 17 February 2015,[8] highlights that provisions to the fund must be coordinated with the provisions of the Italian Civil Code on the automatic dissolution of the company whose capital has fallen below the legal limit, which entitles the entity to decide, based on a prognostic judgment on the future profitability of the company, whether to provide for the reintegration of the share capital or to take note of the automatic liquidation of the body (Articles 2484, paragraph 1, No. 4 and 2447 CC).

To be specific, the Art. 14 d. Decree 175/2016 establishes the prohibition for public authorities to carry out capital increases, extraordinary transfers, credit facilities, or issue guarantees in favor of subsidiaries, with the exception of listed companies and banks, who have registered for three consecutive financial statements and losses for the year or that have used reserves available for the settlement of losses also during the year.

The local partner institution can intervene in the area of losses:

- Only within the limits of its participation in the share capital and cannot provide additional resources.

- Only if the financial intervention is compatible with the provisions of the Community law **on state aid**.

Local administrations will be able to intervene for losses only against companies responsible for the performance of the *service of general economic interest*.

Therefore, the local public administration can make the losses of an investee company with the resources set aside in the restricted fund, within the limits of its shareholding and only after the compatibility with the state aid legislation has been assessed.

It should, however, be kept in mind that **the provision for losses** is a prudential budget rule, so that the entities that have set aside resources cannot, however, freely repay the losses of the investee companies and must instead comply with the requirements indicated in the same paragraph 5 of the aforementioned article 14 of

[8] http://www.quotidianoentilocali.ilsole24ore.com/pa24.php?idDoc=16742623&idDocType=3.

the single text, so any intervention in this sense can only take place within a restructuring plan that guarantees the future balance of the subsidiary's accounts.

Legislative Decree n. 100/2017, conforming to the indications given by the Council of State in its opinion, has also added a paragraph 3-bis to the aforementioned article 21 of d. lgs. n. 175/2016, under which the participating local public administrations can proceed to the level of the losses suffered by the investee company with the sum set aside, within the limits of their shareholding and in compliance with the principles and legislation of the European Union in terms of **state aid**. This means that, on the one hand, the local partner body (beyond the amount of amounts entrusted to an investee for the performance of certain services) can intervene in the level of losses only within the limits of its participation in the share capital and cannot provide additional resources and, on the other hand, that a local public administration can proceed only if the financial intervention is compatible with the provisions of the Community law on state aid: this compatibility is defined by the decision of the EU Commission of December 20, 2011, which codifies the principles established by the ruling judgment on the Altmark case to exclude that a public intervention is an improper aid, conflicting with Article 107 of the EU Treaty.

Consequently, local administrations will be able to intervene for losses only against companies responsible for the performance of the **service of general economic interest** (e.g., transport companies), to offset the service obligations imposed on them and only to condition that the four principles of the Altmark judgment are respected:

a. The recipient undertaking must have been effectively entrusted with the fulfillment of public service obligations, and those obligations must be clearly defined.

b. The parameters on the basis of which the compensation is calculated must be established in advance in an objective and transparent manner.

c. The compensation cannot exceed what is necessary to cover all or part of the costs arising from the fulfillment of the public service obligations, taking into account the relevant revenue and a reasonable profit.

d. The choice of the company to be entrusted with the fulfillment of public service obligations must be made in the context of a public procedure that allows to select the candidate able to provide these services at the **lowest cost for the community**. If the choice of the company, in a specific case, takes place outside of such a procedure, the compensation must be determined on the basis of a cost analysis that should be borne by a medium-sized company, efficiently managed and adequately equipped with means to carry out the service.

With regard to the methods for **hedging the financial resources** allocated to recapitalization and/or loss coverage of investee companies: Art. 3 paragraph 18 of the Budget Law 2004 stipulates that the bodies No *on can borrow to finance contributions aimed at the recapitalization of companies or companies aimed at covering of losses.*

The Court of Auditors[9] (Regional section Abruzzo, sent. No. 1/08) stated that the costs of covering of losses and recapitalizations of participatory bodies should be considered **current expenditure**, and, as such, be taken into account in the calculation of the fund balances.

[9] http://www.corteconti.it/export/sites/portalecdc/_documenti/controllo/abruzzo/pronunce/2017/delibera_115_2017_e_relazione.pdf.

7. Conclusions

The use of corporations by local administrations has been consolidated since the beginning of the nineties of the last century. Since the beginning of the twentieth century, the phenomenon of public intervention in the country's economy had spread, as the corporate phenomenon developed in public administrations, in the absence of specific rules, the belief that the joint-stock company as an organism governed by the civil code was exempted from the application of accounting rules and public finance of public bodies.

The results of the deductive phase have shown that the public investee companies are called to identify new methodologies to direct and control the action of their actions in order to prevent company crises and reorganization.

The provisions of Legislative Decree 175/2016 urge the governance bodies of the public investee companies to use the best and most adequate instruments for monitoring and evaluation with a view to promptly emerge the business crisis. From an economic-business point of view, it can be seen that insolvency can be ascertained mainly ex-post also from outside and through accounting and/or final data 91; on the contrary, the crisis, which has not yet crystallized, giving rise to insolvency, presupposes a vision that is no longer historical but prospective, aimed at identifying the incapacity in the future of fulfilling not only the obligations already assumed but also those foreseeable in the normal course of business.

This suggests considering the possibility of using accounting and/or historical data but with a view to their ability to signal future imbalances, since the accounting indicators examined individually are not very significant for this purpose, that is, without adequate spatial comparison, time and a joint analysis with *ratios,* and operating results in the multiple economic-financial-equity aspects of the investee company.

Consistently with what is outlined by the economic-business doctrine on the uncertainty that distinguishes the identification of an actual state of crisis, there is a need to always combine qualitative information with the most immediate accounting quantitative data and to accompany simple historical analysis, results with a thorough examination of the future action plans, and the related forecast financial and economic flows.

The analysis shows that the legislator has provided a fairly adequate instrumentation (fund for investee losses) only after the losses have been produced. Here it is considered that preference should be given to a prospective and planning perspective. Basically, only a medium-term planning can effectively detect a state of crisis, confirming its finality or anticipating the outcomes; therefore, the introduction of such an approach would give rise to an extremely useful planning logic for the public investee companies.

Author details

Pina Puntillo
Department of Business Administration and Law, University of Calabria, Cosenza, Italy

*Address all correspondence to: pina.puntillo@unical.it

References

[1] Broadbent J, Guthrie J. Changes in the public sector: A review of recent 'alternative' accounting research. Accounting, Auditing & Accountability Journal. 1992;**5**(2):3-31

[2] Puntillo P. Inter-municipal cooperation in service delivery and governance: Insights from Italy. International Journal of Business Governance and Ethics. 2017;**12**(3):197-217

[3] Del Bello A. Intangibles and sustainability in local government reports: An analysis into an uneasy relationship. Journal of Intellectual Capital. 2006;**7**(4):440-456

[4] Bossi A, Fuentes Y, Serrano C. Reflexiones en torno a la aplicacion del capital intelectual en el sector publico. Revista Espanola de Financiacion y Contabilidad. 2005;**XXXIV**(124):211-245

[5] Joyce P. Strategic Management for the Public Services. UK: McGraw-Hill Education; 1999

[6] Bossi A. La medicion del capital intelectual en el sector publico [doctoral dissertation]. Zaragoza: University of Zaragoza; 2003 (summary in Revista Espanola de Financiacion y Contabilidad, Vol XXXII No. 118, pp. 921-5)

[7] Carlin TM. Debating the impact of accrual accounting and reporting in the public sector. Financial Accountability & Management. 2005;**21**(3):309-336

[8] Hodges R, Mellet H. Testing the new public management: Accounting regulation and due process. Paper for presentation at The European Accounting Association Congress; 2002

[9] Mouritsen J et al. Intellectual capital and new public management: Reintroducing enterprise. The Learning Organization. 2004;**11**(4-5):380-392

[10] Hood C. The new public management' in the 1980s: Variation on a theme. Accounting Organizations and Society. 1995;**20**(2-3):93-109

[11] Olsen JP, Guy Peters B, editors. Lessons from Experience: Experiential Learning in Administrative Reforms in Eight Democracies. Oslo: Scandinavian University Press; 1996

[12] EFQM. Common interest day workshops—Management of innovation. Quality Link. 1997;**9**(51):7-11